KITCHEN BASICS

BON APPETIT PUBLISHING CORP.
PUBLISHER

LOS ANGELES

INTRODUCTION

As we race toward the end of the twentieth century, culinary experts are hard at work trying to define the cooking and dining trends that will carry us on into the new millennium.

While opinions may vary on some fine points, there appears to be a consensus on three basic trends. First is a continuing emphasis on lighter, fresher, healthier ingredients and methods of preparation that reflects a realization that part of the pleasure of good cooking is the contribution it makes to our general well-being. And, with the world continuing to shrink, the cooking of the future will continue to embrace the best methods, preparations and ingredients of the world's cuisines. At the same time, the third trend for the new century is a return to basic, home-style cooking—with, of course, a new emphasis on freshness and lightness, and enlivened by the wide range of exotic new ingredients that are fast becoming supermarket staples.

Bearing these trends in mind, this two-book set–taken from the pages of *Bon Appétit* magazine—offers a comprehensive guide, with recipes, to the kitchen trends, skills and recipes that will lead us into the coming century. The first volume covers the basic information any good cook needs at his or her fingertips today—from stocking the pantry to selecting the perfect seasoning, storing foods to substituting ingredients to choosing the perfect wine to accompany a meal.

This basics-oriented approach is reflected in the second volume's techniques and recipes. Each of the chapters here begins with a brief discussion of the essential techniques involved, along with the tips and hints that lead to their mastery and to producing the lightest, healthiest cooking possible. The recipes that illustrate these techniques and tips combine the best of the world's cuisines with the very best of honest-to-goodness, all-American cooking. Use the two volumes together or separately to inform, enlighten and inspire you in your own culinary efforts.

We're proud and pleased to offer you this unique kitchen compendium. Enjoy it and, in a time-honored culinary greeting, "*Bon Appétit!*"

Published by Bon Appétit Publishing Corp., a subsidiary of Knapp Communications Corporation. 5900 Wilshire Boulevard, Los Angeles, California 90036.

Printed and bound in the United States of America.

Cover Photograph by Kathlene Persoff

CONTENTS

VOLUME ONE

CONTENTS

THE WELL-STOCKED PANTRY

Use this checklist as a guide to stocking your kitchen shelves, refrigerator and freezer. Add fresh produce, meat, poultry and seafoods—and the odd special gourmet or ethnic item—and you're well set to tackle most any recipe.

BREADS, GRAINS AND BEANS

- Breads (may be frozen)
  - Whole-wheat
  - Pita
  - Sourdough
  - French
  - Italian
  - Rolls
- Breadcrumbs (may be frozen)
- Crackers
- Dried beans and pulses
  - Garbanzo
  - Kidney
  - Lentils
  - Navy or white beans
- Flours
  - All-purpose
  - Self-rising
  - Whole-wheat
- Old-fashioned oats
- Pasta and noodles
  - Spaghetti
  - Fettuccini
  - Spinach pasta
  - Egg noodles
- Rice
  - White
  - Brown
- Tortillas

HERBS AND SPICES

See pages 4-8.

PREPARED SAUCES AND CONDIMENTS

- Catsup
- Chili sauce
- Cornstarch
- Dried Garlic
- Gravies
  - Beef
  - Mushroom

PREPARED SAUCES AND CONDIMENTS

- Hot pepper sauce
- Mayonnaise
- Mustard
  - Dry
  - Prepared
  - Dijon-style

- Olive oil
- Salad dressing
- Soy sauce
- Spaghetti sauce
- Steak sauce
- Tomato paste
- Tomato sauce
- Vinegars
  - White
  - Red wine
  - White wine
  - Tarragon
  - Cider
- Worcestershire sauce

FROZEN OR CANNED FOODS

- Sausages
- Seafood
  - Crabmeat
  - Salmon
  - Shrimp
  - Tuna
- Biscuits
- Breads
- Phyllo or strudel dough
- Pie shells
- Puff pastry shells
- Lemon juice concentrate
- Orange juice concentrate
- Artichoke hearts
- Bamboo shoots
- Broths
  - Beef
  - Chicken
  - Seafood
- Chinese pea pods
- Clam juice
- Corn
- Green chilies
- Hearts of palm
- Italian tomatoes
- Kidney beans
- Olives
- Water chestnuts

BAKING AND DESSERTS ESSENTIALS

- Baking powder
- Baking soda
- Chocolates
  - Baking chocolate
  - Semisweet chocolate morsels

THE WELL-STOCKED PANTRY

BAKING AND DESSERTS ESSENTIALS

- Unsweetened cocoa powder
- White chocolate
- Coconut
- Condensed and evaporated milk
- Corn syrup
- Gelatin
- Honey
- Instant coffee powder
- Jams, jellies and preserves
- Maple syrup
- Molasses
- Nuts
  - Almonds
  - Hazelnuts or filberts
  - Pecans
  - Peanuts
  - Pine nuts
  - Pistachios
  - Walnuts
- Oils
  - Vegetable
  - Peanut
- Raisins
- Solid vegetable shortening
- Sugars
  - Granulated
  - Brown
  - Powdered or confectioners'
- Vanilla extract
- Yeast

DAIRY PRODUCTS

- Butter
  - Unsalted
  - Salted
- Cheeses
  - Cheddar
  - Cream cheese
  - Monterey Jack
  - Parmesan
  - Swiss
- Cream
- Eggs
- Milk
- Sour Cream
- Yogurt

WINES, SPIRITS AND LIQUEURS

See page 54.

THE WELL-STOCKED PANTRY

A Guide to Herbs and Spices

Today's versatile cook has close at hand a wide range of seasonings to lend a personal touch to the meals he or she cooks, while opening up the possibility of an almost infinite variety of exciting flavor combinations.

These brief descriptions offer a quick reference guide to the characteristics of the most common—as well as some uncommon—kitchen herbs and spices, along with some suggestions on the kinds of foods each seasoning best enhances. But their guidance, in the end, is necessarily subjective, and it is no substitute for the experience of cooking with and tasting these seasonings yourself—deciding which ones you want to make a regular part of your own kitchen.

BASIL. Delicate and spicy-sweet, this herb—both fresh and dried—is an essential part of Italian cuisine, and also enjoys popularity in French kitchens. Excellent with tomato sauces or salads, and an integral part of the classic pesto sauce.

BAY LEAVES. The whole, dried leaves of the bay laurel tree add their pungent and spicy perfume to most savory, simmered dishes—soups, stews and braises—as well as to pickling mixtures, marinades, and even custards.

CARAWAY SEEDS. A popular spice in Eastern Europe, these small, whole, crescent-shaped seeds flavor sausages, sauerkraut, roasts, stews, cheese dishes and baked goods—including the classic rye bread.

CARDAMON. Sold either as whole, small pods or ground into a powder, this sweet spice seasons desserts as well as savory Indian dishes.

CAYENNE PEPPER. Ground from a hot blend of dried chili peppers, this fine red powder adds fire to the dishes of many cuisines, including Cajun, Creole and Indian.

CELERY SEEDS. Like the familiar vegetable that grows from them, these seeds have a refreshing, faintly bitter flavor that enhances salads, soups and vegetable dishes.

CHERVIL. This herb's mild flavor is reminiscent of both parsley and anise. Excellent in soups, salads, sauces or egg dishes.

CHILIES. A wide range of different peppers *(see sidebar)* add strong or mild spice and subtle sweetness to any number of savory dishes. In addition, crushed red pepper flakes spark Italian and Southwestern dishes; and pulverized chili powder, a blend of chilies and other seasonings, flavors Southwestern and Mexican dishes such as chili con carne.

CHIVES. Though available dried, this mild-and-sweet, oniony herb is at its best fresh, snipped as a seasoning or garnish for dairy and egg dishes, salads, soups, seafood, poultry and vegetables.

CILANTRO. Used fresh, this refreshingly spicy herb—which resembles broad-leafed Italian parsley—is a frequent seasoning in Mexican, Chinese and Indian dishes.

KNOW YOUR CHILIES...

Chilies come in such a vast array of types that it would be impossible to list them all here. Additionally, they tend to cross-fertilize, so there can be unexpected variations within each species. To confuse matters further, the same chili sometimes goes under a different name depending on locale.

Basically, chilies are divided into the dried red type and the green variety (usually employed fresh, canned or pickled). The following glossary should help identify similar varieties, so you can choose appropriate substitutes.

REDS (Dried)

ANCHO: This is the all-purpose dried red chili. It is about 2 to 5 inches long, broad, full flavored and rather mild. Fresh, it's the chili *poblano.*

MULATO: Same shape as the *ancho*, but brownish black in color, a little larger and with a sweeter flavor.

PASILLA: About 7 inches long, very dark red and more

continued on next page

HERBS AND SPICES

continued from page 5

KNOW YOUR CHILIES...

pungent, though not as rich in flavor as either the *ancho* or *mulato.* Fresh, it's the chili *chilaca.*

CHIPOTLE: Light brown, smoked, about 2¾ inches long, it is the ripened, dried *jalapeño.* It's very hot.

GREENS (Fresh, Canned)

ANAHEIM: Long green chili, mild, also called California green chili. When canned, labeled "green chili."

SERRANO: A small, tapering all-purpose mild green chili sold fresh or canned. The fresh, long chili *cayenne* can be substituted if *serrano* unavailable.

POBLANO: This is dark green, can be mild or hot. Not readily available in the United States. Use canned, peeled green chilies as a substitute.

JALAPEÑO: This small, green hot chili is available fresh in California and the Southwest as well as canned in other parts of the country.

GÜERO: A very pale yellowish chili, the *güero* averages 4 to 5 inches, can vary from hot to very hot. Available canned from California.

CINNAMON. This sweet, lively spice flavors desserts—and, occasionally, main dishes—worldwide. Stick cinnamon is added to stews, pilafs, pickling mixtures, and mulled wine and cider. Powdered cinnamon is wonderful in apple recipes, baked goods, and as a flavoring for coffee and tea.

CLOVES. Rich and aromatic, these dried flower buds are added whole to pickling brines, and stud many a holiday ham. Ground cloves are a favorite dessert spice—especially as a companion to cinnamon in apple pies.

CORIANDER. Whole or ground, these spicy-sweet seeds season many Middle Eastern dishes, and are an important element of Indian curries.

CUMIN. Strong, pungent and slightly musty, whole or ground cumin seeds spice up a host of savory Mexican, Middle Eastern and Indian recipes.

CURRY POWDER. This blend of spices—including cardamon, chilies, coriander, cumin and turmeric—is a standby of Indian cooking. Some recipes may call for you to use a ready-made blend; others may call for blending your own from specific combinations of seasonings.

HERBS AND SPICES

DILL. Fresh or dried, this feathery-leafed herb has a sweet perfume that goes well with pickles, vinegars, salads, vegetables, seafood, chicken, veal and pork.

GINGER. Sweet and spicy, fresh ginger root is a frequent ingredient in Asian recipes. Dried and powdered ginger enhances many classic cake and cookie recipes, as well as other desserts.

MACE. The dried and ground outer husk of the nutmeg, mace has a subtler flavor than that spice and is in dessert-making and baking.

MARJORAM. Used frequently but sparingly, this pungent, highly aromatic herb is especially good with lamb, and also flavors other meat, poultry and seafood dishes as well as various sauces, soups, vegetables, and egg recipes.

MINT. Fresh mint leaves add their lively, refreshing taste to a classic sauce for roast lamb, as well as to peas, fruit salads and hot or iced tea.

MUSTARD. Whole mustard seeds lend their pungency to pickling brines. Whole or ground mustard, besides being the base of the popular condiment, enlivens sauces for meat, poultry, seafood or vegetables.

NUTMEG. Rich, sweet and aromatic, nutmeg—used already ground or freshly grated—adds complex flavor to desserts (particularly apple pie) as well as savory seafood, poultry, meat or vegetable dishes.

OREGANO. Pungent and aromatic, this herb—used dried or fresh—is popular in Italian, Greek and southern French cuisines as a seasoning for sauces, all manner of main courses, and vegetables.

PAPRIKA. Ground from dried, sweet red peppers, this popular seasoning adds rich flavor and brick-red color to seafood, poultry and meat dishes—particularly those of Hungary and Spain.

PARSLEY. This essential kitchen herb should always be used fresh to flavor sauces, stews, soups, salads, eggs, and all manner of main courses. The broad- flat-leafed Italian variety has a much more distinctive flavor than the more familiar crinkly-leafed kind.

PEPPERCORNS. Black pepper adds its bold spark to savory foods in the kitchen or on the dining table. White peppercorns—from which the dark outer husks have been removed—have

HERBS AND SPICES

a somewhat more subtle flavor and are often used with light-colored foods or sauces whose appearance might be marred by black pepper. While ground pepper is available, it is always best to buy whole peppercorns and grind your own as needed with a pepper mill.

ROSEMARY. Either fresh or dried, rosemary's strong, aromatic flavor is a natural with lamb and veal, as well as with poultry, seafood and vegetables—particularly roast potatoes.

SAFFRON. As precious and costly as gold dust, just a slight sprinkling of this spice—the dried stamens of a species of crocus—impart a beguiling perfume and a bright yellow color to such classic dishes as Spanish paella, French bouillabaisse and Indian pilafs.

SAGE. This very pungent herb is a popular seasoning for pork, ham, sausages, lamb and chicken, a frequent addition to stuffings, and also flavors robust seafood dishes.

TARRAGON. Sweet, savory and very aromatic, this herb—either fresh or dried—flavors egg dishes, seafood, poultry, light meats, and vegetables. It's also a classic flavoring for white wine vinegar used in vinaigrette dressings.

THYME. Distinctively aromatic, with a crisp, strong taste and fragrance, this classic herb seasons poultry, light meats, seafood and eggs.

TURMERIC. While its flavor is pungent and earthy, this ground spice adds—like saffron—a bright yellow color to whatever dishes it seasons.

BASIC STOCKS AND SAUCES

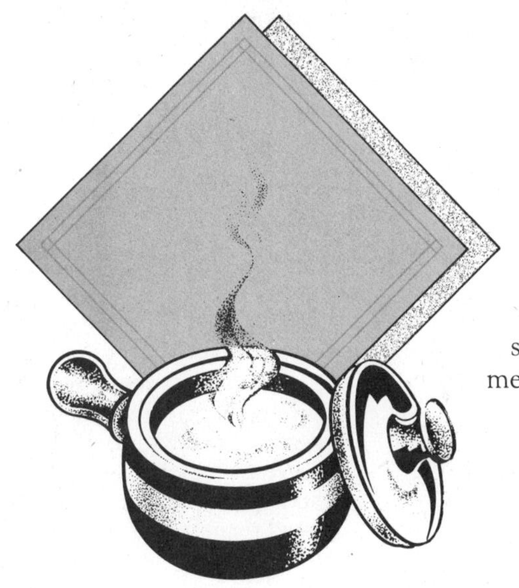

Good cooks depend on a few very basic preparations to form the foundation of a wide range of dishes. A supply of full-flavored stocks—and the skills to prepare several simple, flavorful sauces—will help to ensure a large measure of culinary success.

Use the following recipes as the starting point for your own ever-growing kitchen repertoire.

MEAT OR CHICKEN STOCK

This classic stock, made from chicken—or a mixture of chicken and beef—simmered with vegetables, herbs and spices, is one of the cook's most dependable staples. It has dozens of uses: It is perfect poaching liquid; it is the basis for many sauces; it can be converted into a classic French pot-au-feu with the addition of meat and fresh vegetables. A little cream and vegetable puree transform it into any number of smooth, flavorful soups; and clarified with egg white, it becomes a shimmering broth.

Although it can be made with chicken alone—substituting 2 pounds of chicken bones and 3 more pounds of chicken for the beef bones and beef—beef adds richness and body, and the long simmering process mingles and concentrates the flavors. Consommé freezes well and will keep in the refrigerator for up to a week.

The stock should be prepared ahead and chilled to facilitate removal of fat. It will keep in the refrigerator a minimum of 3 days. After 3 days, either bring to boil and rechill or freeze in batches. An empty milk carton is a good freezer container.

Makes 3 to 4 quarts

Meats

2 pounds beef soup bones
2 pounds chicken bones, giblets and backs
3 pounds beef (stew meat, short ribs or chuck)
1 3-pound fryer chicken, cut in half lengthwise

Vegetables

3 stalks celery with leaves
3 carrots, unpeeled, scrubbed
3 leeks, cleaned and split (reserve green tops)
1 large onion, unpeeled, root end removed
2 parsnips or turnips
6 parsley sprigs
5 garlic cloves, unpeeled, lightly crushed

Seasonings

3 sprigs fresh dill or 2 teaspoons dried
1 teaspoon thyme
2 bay leaves
6 whole cloves
1 teaspoon whole allspice
3 ⅛-inch slices fresh ginger or 1 teaspoon ground
1 teaspoon peppercorns
2 teaspoons salt

Arrange beef and chicken bones in bottom of 12- to 16-quart stockpot. Add beef, celery, carrots, leeks (white part only), onion, parsnips or turnips, parsley, garlic, and seasonings. Add enough cold water to cover ¾ of contents. Slowly bring to a simmer and cook uncovered 1 hour.

Add chicken halves and cover soup with green leek tops to keep flavors from evaporating. Simmer 1 hour longer or until soup has a rich flavor.

Let vegetables and meat cool in broth. When cool, remove meat and bones. Reserve meat. With a wooden spoon press vegetables through strainer, returning juices to soup. Strain broth into 6-quart bowl or pan. Return meat to broth. Refrigerate overnight.

Discard solid layer of fat on top of chilled soup. Reheat stock and season to taste with salt and pepper.

BASIC STOCKS AND SAUCES

BASIC FISH STOCK

As seafood takes on an increasingly important role in the kitchen, so does fish stock (called *fumet* by the French). With a supply of good fish stock in the freezer, the number of seafood recipes in the cook's repertoire multiplies dramatically. It serves as a rich, savory broth for poaching fish and shellfish and as a delectable base for sauces, such as the classic fish *velouté*. It's an indispensable ingredient in many aspics and soups.

Making your own fumet is a simple, speedy process (simmering time is only 35 minutes), once the shopping is completed. A good stock requires absolutely fresh fish bones, trimmings and heads (these contribute body). Since fish markets usually discard these parts right away, it is necessary to order them in advance. Most fish markets will clean the bones and cut them up for a small fee. The best fish to use for this purpose are the lean white varieties—halibut, cod, haddock, sole, pike and flounder—rather than the oily, strong-flavored species, such as mackerel, skate, mullet and bluefish. Salmon can be used, but because it has such a distinctive flavor, any stock made with it should be strictly limited to salmon dishes.

Before using for a sauce or soup, boil fish stock and reduce to intensify flavor. Add salt only after reducing stock and combining it with other ingredients.

Makes about 1 quart

3 pounds fish bones (heads, frames, trimmings), rinsed, dried and cut into 3-inch pieces
2 tablespoons (¼ stick) butter
1 leek (white part only), sliced
1 small carrot, sliced
1 small celery stalk (with leaves), sliced
2 ounces mushroom stems (optional)
10 parsley sprigs (with stems)
6 fresh thyme sprigs or 2 teaspoons dried thyme, crumbled
½ bay leaf
6 white peppercorns, coarsely crushed
3 1½-inch strips lemon peel
2 cups dry white wine
5 cups (about) cold water

Discard any feathery red gills from fish heads if necessary (this will prevent stock from tasting bitter). Melt butter in heavy nonaluminum 8-quart pot over low heat. Add fish and next 7 ingredients. Cover and cook, stirring occasionally, until vegetables are translucent, about 10 minutes. Add peppercorns and lemon peel and blend well. Pour in wine and enough water just to cover ingredients (liquids should not be warm or juices will be sealed in rather than extracted). Bring mixture slowly to simmering point. Partially cover pan and reduce heat until liquid is just shaking (do not boil or stock will be cloudy). Cook, skimming foam from surface as necessary, until stock is richly flavored, about 35 minutes.

Line fine sieve or strainer with several layers of dampened cheesecloth and set

BASIC STOCKS AND SAUCES

over large bowl. Strain stock into bowl, pressing down lightly on fish and vegetables with back of spoon to extract as much liquid as possible. Let cool. Refrigerate. Discard fat that accumulates on surface. Store stock in refrigerator, or freeze. If refrigerating, reboil every 3 days to prevent spoilage.

Recipe can be halved or doubled.

CLARIFIED STOCK

Clarification removes free-floating particles from stock, leaving it clear and sparkling, a necessary procedure for a beautiful aspic but an optional refinement for soups or sauces. To clarify stock, combine 2 egg whites and 1 crushed egg shell in heavy 2-quart saucepan. Gradually whisk in 1 quart of cold, fat-free stock. Place over medium-high heat and stir just until stock reaches a boil. Reduce heat and simmer 15 minutes. Gently ladle stock through fine sieve or strainer lined with dampened dish towel or cheesecloth.

THICKENING AGENTS

The proper thickening of a sauce or gravy is one of the most basic of cooking skills. Gravies are thickened, or "bound," with starches such as arrowroot, cornstarch, flour or potato flour. Sauces can also be thickened with starch alone; with a mixture of flour and fat (when cooked, this is called a *roux*, when uncooked, a *beurre manié*); with a protein such as egg yolk; by reduction; and with pureed vegetables.

STARCHES

Different starches produce different results; you should be aware of the effects of each before making a sauce or gravy.

FLOUR is used to thicken opaque sauces, such as the classic béchamel and velouté, and gravies. It is customarily mixed with a fat of some sort (butter and meat juices are common) and can be either cooked or uncooked.

Flour and fat cooked together form a ***roux,*** which is the first step in the preparation of a number of classic sauces. The proportion of butter to flour in a roux is generally one to one, but the proportion of liquid to flour varies depending on the sauce and its intended use. A rule of thumb:

1 tablespoon flour + 1 cup liquid = thin consistency ideal for soups

2 tablespoons flour + 1 cup liquid = medium consistency correct for cream sauces

3 tablespoons flour + 1 cup liquid = thick consistency appropriate for soufflé bases

Keep in mind, however, that the thickness of the liquid also affects the consistency of the final product. Heavy cream will require less flour than will stock to attain the same consistency.

THICKENING AGENTS

Cook a roux in a small, heavy saucepan. This is important since it will allow the butter to heat slowly, so that when the flour is added the starch granules will expand. If the butter is too hot when the flour is added, the starch granules will shrink, causing lumps and a bitter flavor. In the absence of a heavy saucepan, use a heat diffuser.

To make a white roux for a béchamel or velouté, heat butter until foam has almost disappeared. Remove pan from heat and whisk in flour. Return pan to medium-low heat, whisking constantly until mixture resembles a honeycomb and is a pale, strawlike color—this should take approximately two minutes for each two tablespoons of butter and flour. Cooking the flour eliminates any raw, starchy flavor from the finished sauce. To make a golden roux, used in the preparation of soufflés and some veloutés, cook the roux approximately four minutes for each two tablespoons of butter and flour, or until it is pale golden in color. A brown roux, for brown sauces, is cooked until it turns a rich, even brown and has a nutty aroma.

A raw, or uncooked, roux, ***beurre manié,*** quickly thickens sauces made with poaching or braising liquids. It is a kitchen lifesaver, often used to rescue sauces that for one reason or another have failed to thicken properly. To make it: Mix one part softened butter with two parts flour. Form into balls the size of large peas. Add them a few at a time to a warm sauce or pan juices, over low heat, and stir until sauce is thick and smooth. In general, use 1 tablespoon beurre manié to 1 cup of liquid for a thin sauce; 2 tablespoons to a cup for a medium-thick sauce.

CORNSTARCH, ARROWROOT AND POTATO FLOUR all produce sauces with a translucent appearance, which makes them popular in French cuisine for coating poultry and for thickening fruit sauces. Unlike flour, they contain very little protein. Their individual properties will be discussed below, but they are treated similarly in cooking. They are usually added at the end of the recipe's preparation. The general rule is to dissolve the starch in a small amount of cold liquid, preferably the same liquid used to make the sauce (wine, stock, milk, water) in the proportion of one teaspoon starch to one tablespoon cold liquid. This is called a slurry. Add a few tablespoons of the hot sauce to the slurry to warm it, then, slowly add the warm slurry to the sauce, stirring gently and constantly with spoon until sauce thickens.

CORNSTARCH is a purified floury meal ground from white corn. It can be used in place of flour (1 tablespoon is equivalent

BASIC STOCKS AND SAUCES

THICKENING AGENTS

to 2 tablespoons flour). It is commonly used in puddings, pie fillings, fruit sauces, low-calorie and Oriental cooking. In fact, it is the only thickener used in Chinese cooking. The cornstarch-based sauce is more translucent than that produced by using flour, but not as clear as a sauce made with arrowroot. Do not use cornstarch when high temperature and extended cooking time are called for in the recipe.

ARROWROOT is obtained by drying and grinding the rootstalks of a tropical plant of the same name. It is used primarily when the finished sauce should be clear and transparent. Many chefs prefer arrowroot for last-minute thickening because it leaves no floury aftertaste. It is added to the sauce in the form of a slurry, when cooked with a minimum of stirring until the sauce is clear. Use about one tablespoon to ¾ to one cup of liquid for a medium-thick sauce. Sauces thickened with arrowroot reach their maximum thickness below the boiling point—at 158°F to 176°F. Further heating causes thinning. Excellent for fruit sauces and fruit tarts.

POTATO FLOUR, also known as potato starch, is, not surprisingly, made from potatoes. Like cornstarch, it can be used in place of flour (1 tablespoon is equivalent to 2 tablespoons flour).

EGG YOLK

If egg yolk is the only thickener, use 2 or 3 yolks for each cup of liquid, or a liaison of 2 yolks and 3 tablespoons crème fraîche. Stir yolks to break them up, then gradually add a small amount of hot liquid, stirring constantly, until yolks are warmed. Return egg mixture to the hot liquid in the pan. Stir over low heat until mixture coats a spoon, using a double boiler or a heat diffuser if necessary to control heat. Sauces thickened with egg yolk must be made just before serving and watched very carefully to prevent curdling.

REDUCTION

Thickening a liquid by cooking it uncovered over high heat until the desired consistency is achieved is called reduction. A by-product of this process is concentration of flavors. When a recipe calls for reducing the amount of a liquid by half, do not use guesswork unless your eye is trained to judge amounts. Pour the liquid into a measuring cup and take note of the amount. Return to pan and cook until you think it is sufficiently reduced. Then return the liquid to the measuring cup to double-check. If you have over-reduced, add water to dilute. *Note:* Because reduction intensifies flavor,

BASIC STOCKS AND SAUCES

THICKENING AGENTS

do not season the liquid before reducing. Taste when the correct consistency has been reached and then season. As a general rule, all sauces benefit from some cooking down and concentration of flavor; that is why the yield of a recipe is often less than the total of liquid called for.

PUREED VEGETABLES

Vegetables used in preparing soups or sauces, or a mirepoix cooked with a roast can be strained and pureed in a food processor or blender, then used to thicken the soup or sauce.

ALL-PURPOSE TOMATO SAUCE

A fairly thin sauce is required for baked dishes such as lasagne, as the sauce thickens while it bakes. If a thicker sauce is desired to toss with pasta, for example, do not add the final ⅓ cup of the canned chicken broth.

Makes 3 cups

1½ teaspoons olive oil
1 medium onion, finely chopped
5 garlic cloves, minced
¼ teaspoon dried red pepper flakes
1 bay leaf
1 cup canned low-salt chicken broth, degreased
1 pound plum tomatoes, peeled, seeded and cut into ½-inch dice (about 1½ cups)
1 28-ounce can Italian plum tomatoes, drained and diced (about 1½ cups)
2 teaspoons tomato paste
1 teaspoon sugar (optional)
Salt
Freshly ground pepper

Heat olive oil in heavy large skillet (preferably nonstick) over medium heat. Add onion, garlic, pepper flakes and bay leaf and toss to coat with oil. Add ⅓ cup chicken broth. Cover and cook until onions are tender, stirring occasionally, about 5 minutes. Add fresh and canned tomatoes and tomato paste. Taste and add sugar if desired. Season with salt. Add ⅓ cup chicken broth and cook uncovered until sauce thickens slightly and liquid evaporates, about 15 minutes. Remove bay leaf. Transfer sauce to processor or blender. Add remaining ⅓ cup stock and puree. Season with pepper. *(Can be prepared 2 days ahead. Cover and refrigerate.)*

CLASSIC HOLLANDAISE

Hollandaise heads the family of sauces made by beating butter into thickened warm egg yolks to form a creamy emulsion. All the warm emulsified sauces utilize a small amount of acid to aid in the binding of the egg yolks and butter. Hollandaise calls for lemon juice, which lends a distinctive flavor.

The success of your hollandaise will be assured if the egg yolks are warmed very slowly—which causes them to thicken rather than become scrambled—and if the butter is added gradually. Egg yolks can absorb quite a lot of butter (1 warm yolk will absorb up to 6 tablespoons), but only if it is added very slowly.

Hollandaise traditionally is whisked by hand, but a hand-held electric mixer can be substituted for the whisk. An even simpler version can be whipped up very quickly in a blender or food processor. Either variation may be stored in a tightly closed, wide-necked vacuum bottle that has been preheated with hot water; this will keep the emulsion warm, stable and smooth for hours.

Makes about 1¾ cups

¼ cup water*
1½ tablespoons fresh lemon juice
¼ teaspoon salt
Pinch of freshly ground white pepper

3 egg yolks
1 cup (2 sticks) unsalted butter, melted

Mix water, lemon juice, salt and pepper in small saucepan. Bring to a boil, reduce heat and simmer until liquid is reduced to 2 tablespoons. Set pan in a larger pan of cold water to cool.

Beat yolks in heavy, nonaluminum 1-quart saucepan** until thick and creamy. Slowly beat in lemon reduction. Whisk over very low heat (or beat with electric mixer set on medium speed) until thickened, about 3 to 4 minutes. Do not allow eggs to become too thick or dry. Remove from heat and begin slowly drizzling warm, not hot, melted butter into yolks, beating constantly until all butter has been added and sauce is just pourable. If it is too thick to pour, thin with a little hot water.

**If serving sauce with fish, substitute white wine, dry vermouth or clam juice for water.*

***If a heavy pan is not available, protect the sauce from direct heat by standing pan on a heatproof pad, or over 2 inches of very hot, but not simmering, water. If hollandaise sauce is made in a double boiler, eggs will require about 10 minutes of constant beating to reach the correct consistency.*

BASIC STOCKS AND SAUCES

BLENDER HOLLANDAISE

Makes about ¾ cup

3 egg yolks
2 tablespoons fresh lemon juice
¼ teaspoon salt
⅛ teaspoon cayenne or white pepper
1 tablespoon minced fresh parsley (optional)
½ cup (1 stick) unsalted butter, melted and sizzling hot

Combine yolks, lemon juice, salt, cayenne and parsley (if desired) in blender or food processor and mix 5 seconds. With machine running, pour hot butter into egg mixture in slow steady stream (it should take about 15 seconds). If sauce is too thick, stir in 1 to 2 tablespoons hot water.

MAYONNAISE

Why make your own mayonnaise, when it is so readily available commercially? Quite simply, because the flavor of homemade mayonnaise is incomparable. And it's easy to make. Although mayonnaise is traditionally whisked by hand, the following recipe can be whipped up in short order with an electric mixer. With the help of a blender or food processor, it takes even less time.

Properly stabilized, your mayonnaise will remain fresh and creamy in the refrigerator for at least a week.

All ingredients should be at room temperature or slightly warm.

Makes about 1½ cups

2 egg yolks*
1 teaspoon Dijon mustard, or more to taste
1 tablespoon tarragon or wine vinegar, or lemon juice
⅓ cup olive oil
⅔ cup peanut oil
Salt and white pepper

Mixer or Whisk Method: Place yolks, mustard and vinegar in a large bowl and beat one minute. Add half the oil *very slowly*, drop by drop, beating vigorously and constantly (if oil is added too rapidly, yolks will not completely absorb the oil and the mayonnaise will have a runny consistency). You may add remaining oil by teaspoonfuls, beating constantly. Add salt and white pepper to taste.

Blender or Food Processor Method: Place yolks, mustard, vinegar, salt and pepper in blender, or food processor equipped with steel blade. Turn motor on and immediately begin adding oil in a thin stream. When all oil has been added and mixture has thickened, turn off the machine.

**If using food processor method, 2 whole eggs can be substituted for 2 egg yolks. This will produce a slightly less stiff mayonnaise.*

TO STABILIZE MAYONNAISE:

If homemade mayonnaise is to be stored for more than a day or so, it must

BASIC STOCKS AND SAUCES

be stabilized to prevent separating. For each cup of completed mayonnaise, beat in 2 teaspoons boiling water or stock (chicken or beef).

Store mayonnaise in refrigerator, covering surface with plastic wrap to prevent discoloration.

TO SALVAGE SEPARATED MAYONNAISE:

Use one of these three techniques:

- Put 1 tablespoon mayonnaise into a warm, dry bowl with 1 teaspoon prepared mustard. Whip until creamy. Add remaining mayonnaise a tablespoon at a time, beating vigorously after each addition.
- Substitute 1 tablespoon boiling water for mustard; follow same procedure as above.
- Place a fresh egg yolk in bowl. Beat in separated mixture plus ½ cup oil to balance extra yolk.

BASIC VINAIGRETTE

Vinaigrette, the basic French salad dressing, is a simple combination of oil and vinegar flavored with salt and pepper and sometimes mustard and herbs. In France, it is usually made with wine vinegar, but other vinegars create different flavors, each of which has its distinctive appeal. The choice of oil also influences the flavor of the dressing. Although the traditional ratio of oil to vinegar is 3 to 1, the proportion is strictly a matter of taste, and can range from 4 to 1 to a mixture of 1 to 1. Experimentation is the only way to arrive at the perfect blend.

Makes about ½ cup

1 small to medium garlic clove, peeled
1 teaspoon coarse salt
½ teaspoon freshly ground pepper (white preferred), or to taste
½ teaspoon dry mustard
1 teaspoon Dijon or Düsseldorf mustard
1 egg, beaten, *or* 2 tablespoons whipping cream (optional)*
2 tablespoons olive oil
2 tablespoons tarragon vinegar or wine vinegar
1 teaspoon fresh lemon juice
¼ cup vegetable oil (peanut, corn, safflower, etc.)

Cover cutting surface with a brown paper bag. Place garlic and salt on paper and mince together until they almost form a paste (brown paper absorbs some of the pungent oil, softening the strong garlic flavor). Transfer garlic and salt to mixing bowl. Add pepper, mustards, egg or cream (if desired) and olive oil. Stir vigorously with whisk or wooden spoon. Slowly add vinegar and lemon juice, stirring constantly. Continuing to stir, add vegetable oil drop by drop until all has been absorbed.

**A little egg or cream smooths dressing and keeps it from separating.*

BASIC STOCKS AND SAUCES

BASIC BREADS

We're so used to buying ready-made baked goods—and so many good bakeries are springing up everywhere—that it may at first seem almost pointless to bake your own breads. But home baking offers unlimited variety, marvelous aromas and the satisfaction of producing nourishing, delicious foods with surprising ease. What better reasons could there be to get out the flour and yeast?

FOLLOW THESE GUIDELINES TO HELP YOUR BREADS RISE PERFECTLY TO EVERY OCCASION:

- Calibrate your oven temperature with a good-quality thermometer, and always fully preheat the oven to the required temperature called for in the recipe.
- For higher-rising yeast breads with better crusts, you might want to try lining your oven shelf with baking tiles or a pizza or bread brick—available in good cookware stores—to simulate the radiant heat of the baker's oven.
- Though yeast dough will rise quickly at warm room temperature, generally the longer they take to rise, the better the flavor and texture. So, if time allows, leave doughs to rise at cool room temperature or overnight in the refrigerator.
- When mixing breads or muffins leavened by baking powder, do not overmix the batter. Stir just until the ingredients are moistened, to ensure a tender texture.

SESAME OAT ROLLS

Great with a wedge of cheddar cheese.

Makes 16

2 cups rolled oats
2 cups buttermilk

1½ envelopes dry yeast
¼ cup warm water (105°F to 115°F)

3½ cups (about) unbleached all-purpose flour
¼ cup pure (untoasted) sesame oil or unsalted butter, room temperature
2 teaspoons salt

½ cup sesame seeds

Combine oats and buttermilk in medium bowl. Cover with plastic and refrigerate at least 2 hours or overnight.

Sprinkle yeast over warm water in small bowl; stir to dissolve. Let stand until foamy, about 10 minutes.

Combine oat mixture, 1 cup flour, oil and salt in bowl of heavy-duty mixer (dough can also be mixed by hand). Using paddle attachment, mix on medium speed 2 minutes. Add yeast mixture. Using dough hook, mix in enough flour ½ cup at a time to form soft sticky dough. Knead dough on lightly floured surface until smooth, elastic and slightly sticky, adding more flour if necessary, about 5 minutes.

Grease large bowl. Add dough, turning to coat entire surface. Cover bowl with plastic. Let dough rise in warm area until doubled, about 1½ hours.

Line baking sheet with parchment. Gently punch dough down. Knead on lightly floured surface until smooth. Divide into 16 equal pieces. Shape each piece into ball, pulling edges under to create smooth top. Roll each ball in sesame seeds to coat. Transfer rolls to prepared sheet, spacing 2 inches apart. Cover loosely with plastic and let rise in warm draft-free area until almost doubled in volume, about 30 minutes.

Preheat oven to 400°F. Bake rolls until golden brown, about 30 minutes. Cool slightly on rack before serving.

DO-AHEAD DOUGHS

Fresh, hot homemade dinner rolls can be an every-night thing when the dough's made ahead and refrigerated or frozen. Here's how.

REFRIGERATOR ROLLS *Method One:* After kneading dough, place in greased bowl or large plastic bag. Brush dough with melted solid vegetable shortening or oil. Cover bowl tightly or seal bag, leaving room for dough to rise. Refrigerate up to 4 days, punching dough down once or twice daily if risen.

To serve: Remove the desired amount of dough about 3 hours before serving. Shape, then place on prepared baking sheets or in pans, cover loosely with plastic and let rise until almost doubled, 1½ to 2 hours. Bake as directed.

Method Two: After dough has risen as directed in recipe, shape rolls. Place on prepared baking sheets or in pans and brush with melted butter. Cover loosely with oiled waxed paper, then tightly with plastic wrap. Refrigerate 2 to 24 hours.

To serve: Remove from refrigerator and let stand 20 to 30 minutes. Bake rolls as directed.

FREEZER ROLLS Shape rolls as directed in recipe. Place on nonstick or waxed paper-lined baking sheet that will fit in your freezer. Cover tightly with plastic. Freeze until firm. Transfer to plastic bag. Freeze rolls for up to 1 week.

To serve: Unwrap rolls and place on prepared baking sheet or in pan. Cover loosely with plastic and let come to room temperature and rise in warm draft-free area until almost doubled, 4 to 6 hours. (Dough can also be thawed overnight in refrigerator.) Bake as directed.

BROWN-AND-SERVE ROLLS Shape rolls as directed in recipe. Let rise until almost doubled. Bake at 300°F until set but not browned, about 20 minutes. Cool on rack. Place in plastic bag and refrigerate up to 3 days or freeze up to 3 weeks.

To serve: Let frozen rolls thaw at room temperature. Place rolls on prepared baking sheets or in pans. Bake rolls at 375°F until golden brown, 10 to 15 minutes.

BASIC BREADS

CRUSTY POPPY SEED ROLLS

Quick-rising yeast and food-processor mixing and kneading make these light and crusty rolls an easy and winning addition to almost any meal. Conventional dry yeast can certainly be used, but allow for double the rising times.

Makes 12

- **3 cups (or more) all-purpose flour**
- **1 package fast-rising dry yeast**
- **1½ teaspoons salt**
- **1 cup (or more) hot water (120°F to 130°F)**
- **Yellow cornmeal**
- **1 egg white, beaten with 2 teaspoons water (glaze)**
- **Poppy seeds**

Blend 3 cups flour, yeast and salt in processor fitted with Steel Knife. With machine running, slowly pour 1 cup hot water through feed tube. Process until ball forms. If mixture is too moist to form ball, add additional flour by tablespoons, incorporating each completely before adding the next. If too dry, add hot water by teaspoons, incorporating each before adding next. Knead dough in processor 45 seconds.

Grease large bowl. Add dough, turning to coat entire surface. Cover bowl. Let dough rise in warm draft-free area until doubled, about 35 minutes.

Grease large baking sheet and sprinkle with cornmeal. Punch dough down. Knead on lightly floured surface until smooth, 2 to 3 minutes. Let rest 10 minutes. Divide dough into 12 pieces. Shape each into 2½-inch rounded oval. Place on prepared baking sheet, spacing 2 inches apart. Gently pull rolls to flatten slightly and taper ends with hands. Cover loosely. Let rolls rise in warm draft-free area until almost doubled in volume, about 40 minutes.

Position one rack in lowest third of oven and second rack in center and preheat to 450°F. Place shallow pan of hot water on lower rack. Brush rolls gently with glaze and sprinkle with poppy seeds. Bake in center of oven until golden brown, about 20 minutes. Transfer to rack and cool slightly. *(Can be prepared ahead. Cool completely. Wrap and freeze up to 1 month. Thaw. Rewarm in 350°F oven.)* Serve warm.

POPPY SEED FACTS

Because of their high oil content, poppy seeds do not have a particularly long storage life and can turn rancid. They should be kept in an airtight container. At room temperature they will last about two months, but they will keep longer in the refrigerator—up to a year.

BASIC BREADS

SUN-DRIED TOMATO ROLLS WITH GARLIC

Try these aromatic rolls with Italian pastas, veal dishes and main-course salads.

Makes 12

1 envelope dry yeast
¼ cup sugar
½ cup warm water (105°F to 115°F)

½ cup tomato juice, room temperature
6 tablespoons olive oil or oil from sun-dried tomatoes
2 eggs
1 teaspoon salt
4 cups (about) unbleached all-purpose flour
¼ cup thinly sliced fresh basil
3 tablespoons chopped oil-packed sun-dried tomatoes

Garlic Oil

¼ cup olive oil
2 cloves garlic, pressed

Sprinkle yeast and ¼ teaspoon sugar over warm water in small bowl. Stir to dissolve. Let yeast mixture stand until foamy, about 10 minutes.

Combine remaining sugar, tomato juice, oil, eggs and salt in large bowl. Add 1 cup flour and whisk vigorously for 2 minutes. Add yeast mixture, basil and tomatoes. Mix in enough flour ½ cup at a time to form soft dough. Knead dough on lightly floured surface until smooth and elastic, adding more flour if necessary, about 5 minutes (dough will be slightly sticky).

Grease large bowl. Add dough, turning to coat entire surface. Cover bowl with plastic. Let dough rise in warm area until doubled, about 1 hour.

For garlic oil: Heat oil in small saucepan until just warm. Stir in garlic. Cool.

Lightly grease muffin cups. Gently punch dough down. Knead on lightly floured surface until smooth. Divide into 12 equal pieces. Shape each piece into ball, pulling edges under to create smooth top. Place rolls rounded side up in prepared cups. Using floured scissors, snip ½-inch-deep X into top of each roll. Cover with plastic and let rise in warm draft-free area until doubled in volume, about 20 minutes.

Preheat oven to 375°F. Gently brush rolls with garlic oil. Bake until golden brown, about 20 minutes. Remove rolls from oven and brush again with garlic oil. Transfer rolls to rack and cool slightly before serving.

CHEDDAR CORN ROLLS WITH MUSTARD

These rolls have the subtle tang of mustard and cheddar cheese. They go well with beef brisket, roast beef or poultry.

Makes 18

- **4¼ cups (about) unbleached all-purpose flour**
- **¾ cup cornmeal**
- **3 tablespoons sugar**
- **1 envelope dry yeast**
- **2 teaspoons salt**
- **1¼ cups buttermilk**
- **3 tablespoons unsalted butter or corn oil**
- **2 tablespoons Dijon mustard**
- **2 eggs, room temperature**
- **3 ounces extra-sharp cheddar cheese, shredded (about 1 cup)**

Combine 1 cup all-purpose flour, cornmeal, sugar, yeast and salt in bowl of heavy-duty electric mixer (dough can also be mixed by hand). Heat buttermilk, butter and mustard in medium saucepan to 120°F (mixture may appear curdled). Add to dry ingredients in mixer. Mix with dough hook until smooth and creamy. Add eggs and 1 cup all-purpose flour and mix until well combined. Mix in cheese. Add enough all-purpose flour ½ cup at a time to form soft dough that pulls away from sides of bowl. Knead dough on lightly floured surface until smooth and elastic but slightly sticky, adding more flour only if necessary, about 10 minutes.

Grease large bowl. Add dough, turning to coat entire surface. Cover loosely with plastic wrap. Let dough rise in warm draft-free area until doubled in volume, about 1¼ hours.

Line large baking sheet with parchment. Gently punch dough down. Knead on lightly floured surface until smooth. Divide into 18 pieces. Shape each into smooth ball. Place on baking sheet, spacing 1 inch apart and pressing to flatten. Slash X in center of each. Cover loosely with plastic. Let rolls rise in warm draft-free area until almost doubled in volume, about 45 minutes.

Preheat oven to 375°F. Bake rolls until golden brown, about 18 minutes. Cool slightly on rack before serving.

CARROT CLOVERLEAF ROLLS

This recipe can also be made with cooked, mashed winter squash, such as butternut, acorn or pumpkin. These are delicious with vegetable cream soups, roast onions, stews and roast beef.

Makes 20

- **¾ pound carrots, peeled and cut into ½-inch pieces**
- **1 envelope dry yeast**
- **Pinch of brown sugar**
- **¼ cup warm water (105°F to 115°F)**
- **¾ cup warm milk (105° to 115°F)**
- **6 tablespoons unsalted butter, melted**
- **¼ cup bourbon or dark rum**
- **3 tablespoons brown sugar**
- **1½ tablespoons grated orange peel**
- **1 tablespoon salt**
- **4½ cups (about) unbleached all-purpose flour**
- **1 egg, beaten to blend (glaze)**

Cook carrots in saucepan of simmering water until tender, about 10 minutes. Drain well and pat dry. Puree carrots in processor until smooth.

Sprinkle yeast and pinch of sugar over warm water in small bowl; stir to dissolve. Let yeast mixture stand until foamy, about 10 minutes.

Whisk together 1 cup carrot puree, milk, butter, bourbon, 3 tablespoons sugar, orange peel and salt in large bowl. Add yeast mixture and 2 cups flour. Stir vigorously with wooden spoon until smooth and creamy, about 3 minutes. Mix in enough flour ½ cup at a time to form soft dough. Knead dough on lightly floured surface until smooth and elastic, adding more flour if necessary, about 10 minutes.

Grease large bowl. Add dough, turning to coat entire surface. Cover bowl with plastic. Let dough rise in warm area until doubled, about 1 hour.

Lightly grease 20 muffin cups. Gently punch dough down. Knead on lightly floured surface until smooth. Divide dough into quarters. Divide each quarter into 5 pieces. Divide each piece into 3 smaller pieces. Roll each dough piece on lightly floured surface into 1-inch ball. Place 3 balls in each muffin cup. Cover loosely with plastic and let rise in warm draft-free area until almost doubled, about 30 minutes.

Preheat oven to 400°F. Gently brush rolls with glaze. Bake until golden brown, about 25 minutes. Transfer to rack and cool slightly before serving.

PUMPKIN SEED AND BRAN CRESCENTS

Rich and delightfully chewy. Once you get the hang of rolling the wedges into a crescent shape, it's easy—practice makes perfect. Try them with roast turkey.

Makes 24

1 envelope dry yeast
Pinch of sugar
¼ cup warm water (105°F to 115°F)

1 cup buttermilk
¼ cup (½ stick) unsalted butter, melted
3 tablespoons maple syrup
1 egg
1½ teaspoons salt
¾ cup bran flakes
¾ cup raw pumpkin seeds*
3½ cups (about) unbleached all-purpose flour

Sprinkle yeast and sugar over warm water in small bowl; stir to dissolve. Let stand until foamy, about 10 minutes.

Combine buttermilk, butter, maple syrup, egg and salt in large bowl. Whisk in yeast mixture, bran, pumpkin seeds and 1 cup flour. Stir vigorously until mixture is smooth and creamy, about 3 minutes. Using wooden spoon, mix in enough flour ½ cup at a time to form soft dough. Knead dough on lightly floured surface until smooth and elastic, adding more flour if necessary, approximately 5 minutes.

Grease large bowl. Add dough, turning to coat entire surface. Cover bowl with plastic. Let dough rise in warm area until doubled, about 1 hour.

Line 2 baking sheets with parchment. Gently punch dough down. Knead on lightly floured surface until smooth. Divide into 3 equal pieces. Roll or pat each piece on lightly floured surface into 8-inch circle. Cut each circle into 8 wedges using sharp knife. Roll each up, starting at wide end. Transfer to prepared sheets arranging point side down and spacing 1 inch apart. Curve ends down to form crescents. Cover loosely with plastic and let rise in warm area until almost double in volume, about 20 minutes.

Preheat oven to 350°F. Bake rolls until golden brown, about 25 minutes. Cool slightly on rack before serving.

**Also known as* pepitas. *Available at Latin American markets, natural foods stores and many supermarkets.*

BASIC BREADS

RAISIN WALNUT BREAD

Makes 1 loaf

1 cup raisins
1 cup boiling water

2 cups all-purpose flour
1 cup sugar
1 teaspoon baking soda
¼ teaspoon salt
1 egg, beaten to blend
2 tablespoons margarine, melted
1 teaspoon vanilla
1 teaspoon almond extract
1 cup chopped walnuts

Preheat oven to 375°F. Butter 5x9-inch loaf pan. Place raisins in large bowl. Cover with boiling water. Let stand 10 minutes.

Mix together flour, sugar, baking soda and salt in medium bowl. Add egg, margarine, vanilla and almond extract to raisins and water. Stir in dry ingredients. Mix in walnuts. Pour into prepared pan. Bake until tester inserted in center comes out clean, about 45 minutes. Cool 10 minutes in pan on rack. Invert onto rack and cool completely. *(Can be prepared 1 day ahead. Wrap and chill.)*

OATMEAL RAISIN SCONES

Serve these teatime or breakfast specialties with strawberry jam.

Makes 12

2 cups rolled oats
2 cups sifted all-purpose flour
¼ cup sugar
1 tablespoon baking powder
½ teaspoon baking soda
½ teaspoon salt
6 tablespoons (¾ stick) chilled butter, cut into ½-inch pieces
⅔ cup raisins
1¼ cups (about) buttermilk
Half-and-half
Sugar

Preheat oven to 375°F. Finely grind 1 cup oats in processor. Blend in flour, ¼ cup sugar, baking powder, baking soda and salt. Add butter and cut in until mixture resembles coarse meal, using on/off turns. Transfer to large bowl. Mix in ⅔ cup raisins and remaining 1 cup oats. Make well in center of mixture. Gradually mix in enough buttermilk to form moist dough.

Gently knead dough on lightly floured surface until smooth, about 10 turns. Divide into 3 pieces. Pat each into ¾-inch-thick round on floured surface. Cut each into quarters. Brush with half-and-half and sprinkle with sugar. Transfer to baking sheet. *(Can be prepared 4 hours ahead. Cover and refrigerate.)* Bake until golden brown, about 28 minutes. Serve hot.

BASIC BREADS

GLAZED BRAN MUFFINS

Makes 12

2 tablespoons (¼ stick) butter, room temperature
2 tablespoons sugar
2 tablespoons dark brown sugar
1½ tablespoons honey
1½ tablespoons hot water

1 cup whole wheat flour
½ cup natural bran
½ cup oatmeal
½ cup raisins
1 tablespoon wheat germ
1 teaspoon baking soda
¾ cup milk
½ cup honey
¼ cup vegetable oil
1 egg, beaten to blend
1½ teaspoons light molasses
½ teaspoon vanilla

Preheat oven to 350°F. Using electric mixer, cream butter with both sugars in small bowl. Add honey and water and beat until smooth. Brush 12-cup muffin tin with butter mixture.

Combine flour and next 5 ingredients in medium bowl. Mix milk and next 5 ingredients in large bowl. Add dry ingredients and stir until just combined. Pour batter into prepared muffin cups. Bake until tester inserted in centers comes out clean, about 12 minutes. Turn out onto rack. *(Can be prepared 1 day ahead. Cool. Store airtight.)*

MEASURING FLOUR

Unless a recipe specifies, the best way to measure flour is to spoon it lightly into the measuring cup and level it with a straight-edged spatula or knife. Dipping into the flour tends to compact it, resulting in a different measure than intended. However, if a recipe tells you to use a particular method, follow those instructions so that the final product is what the author intended. Just remember never to tap or shake the cup, as that will also compact the flour.

In fact, the most accurate way to measure flour is to weigh it. But since few American recipes list ingredient weights, the home baker rarely has the opportunity to take advantage of this method.

BASIC BREADS

POWER PEAR-OAT MUFFINS

These satisfying muffins are packed with whole grains, fruits and high-fiber yams. The muffins freeze beautifully for up to 1 month.

Makes 12

- **¾ cup whole wheat flour**
- **½ cup plus 2 tablespoons firmly packed dark brown sugar**
- **⅓ cup finely chopped pitted dates**
- **¼ cup raisins**
- **¼ cup rolled oats**
- **¼ cup sunflower seeds (unsalted), toasted**
- **3 tablespoons oat bran***
- **3 tablespoons toasted wheat germ**
- **1 teaspoon baking soda**
- **1 teaspoon ground allspice**
- **½ teaspoon baking powder**
- **½ teaspoon salt**
- **½ teaspoon ground ginger**
- **½ cup vegetable oil**
- **⅓ cup shredded bran cereal (such as All-Bran)**
- **2 eggs**
- **2 teaspoons vanilla extract**
- **1 large pear, peeled, cored and finely chopped**
- **1 cup grated peeled yam or sweet potato (about 4 ounces)**

Preheat oven to 375°F. Grease twelve ½-cup muffin cups. Mix first 13 ingredients in medium bowl. Combine oil, bran cereal, eggs and vanilla in large bowl. Let stand until bran absorbs liquid, about 3 minutes. Using electric mixer, beat bran cereal mixture until thick. Beat in pear and yam. Fold in dry ingredients; do not overmix (batter will be thick and lumpy).

Divide batter among prepared muffin cups. Bake until tester inserted in centers comes out clean, about 25 minutes. Serve warm. *(Can be prepared ahead. Cool completely on rack. Wrap tightly and refrigerate 3 days, or freeze up to 1 month. Rewarm in 350°F oven.)*

**Available at natural foods stores. Rolled oats can be substituted.*

BASIC BREADS

Just how long *will* that bottle of olive oil keep? Are those eggs that have been in the refrigerator for two weeks getting too old? Is it time to buy a new container of baking powder? Time to toss out those frozen shrimp that seem to have been there forever?

Such storage questions plague most every cook from time to time. The following chart will give you some answers for cupboard and refrigerator storage, and a sidebar addresses the special planning and storage considerations of freezing. But, above all, never substitute what your eyes and nose can tell you about whether a particular food product is worth keeping or destined for disposal.

FRESH PRODUCE

ITEM	HOW TO STORE	MAXIMUM STORAGE TIME
Apples	In refrigerator crisper or a closed bag at cool room temperature	1 month
Asparagus	In refrigerator crisper	3-5 days
Beans & Peas	In pods, in refrigerator crisper	5-7 days
Berries & Cherries	In refrigerator crisper	3-5 days
Broccoli, Cabbage, Cauliflower & Brussels Sprouts	In refrigerator crisper	5-7 days
Citrus fruits	In refrigerator crisper or a closed bag at cool room temperature	2 weeks
Corn on the Cob	In husks, in refrigerator crisper (for maximum sweetness)	1-2 days
Lettuces and other leaves	In vegetable crisper	5 days
Onions	Cool, dark, dry room temperature, with air circulation	1 week
Pineapples	In refrigerator crisper	2 days
Potatoes	Cool, dark, dry room temperature, with air circulation	1 week
Root vegetables	In refrigerator crisper, with leafy tops removed	2 weeks

FRESH PRODUCE

ITEM	HOW TO STORE	MAXIMUM STORAGE TIME
Soft Fruits & Melons	In refrigerator crisper	5 days
Summer Squashes	In refrigerator crisper	1 week
Tomatoes & Cucumbers	In refrigerator crisper	1 week

DAIRY PRODUCTS

ITEM	HOW TO STORE	MAXIMUM STORAGE TIME
Butter	Refrigerated in butter keeper	1 week
Buttermilk	Refrigerated	2 weeks
Cheeses	Tightly wrapped and refrigerated	2 weeks
Cottage & Ricotta Cheeses	Refrigerated, tightly covered	5 days
Cream & Sour Cream	Refrigerated	1 week
Eggs in Shell	Refrigerated in carton	1 month
Egg Whites	Refrigerated in covered container	4 days
Egg Yolks	Refrigerated, covered with water	4 days
Margarine	Refrigerated	1 month
Milk	Refrigerated	1 week
Yogurt	Refrigerated	1 week

STORING FOOD

STORING FOOD

FRESH SEAFOOD, POULTRY AND MEAT

ITEM	HOW TO STORE	MAXIMUM STORAGE TIME
Bacon	Loosely wrapped and refrigerated	1 week
Cold Cuts	Loosely wrapped and refrigerated	5 days
Ground or Stewing Meat	Loosely wrapped and refrigerated	2 days
Ham, sliced	Loosely wrapped and refrigerated	3 days
Ham, whole	Loosely wrapped and refrigerated	1 week
Hot Dogs	Loosely wrapped and refrigerated	1 week
Poultry	Loosely wrapped and refrigerated	2 days
Roasts, Chops & Steaks	Loosely wrapped and refrigerated	5 days
Sausage, dry	Loosely wrapped and refrigerated	2-3 weeks
Sausage, fresh	Loosely wrapped and refrigerated	2 days
Seafood	Tightly wrapped and refrigerated	1 day

LEFTOVERS AND OPENED PACKAGED FOODS

ITEM	HOW TO STORE	MAXIMUM STORAGE TIME
Cakes or Pies, dairy-filled	Tightly covered, refrigerated	2 days
Fruits, cut	Tightly covered, refrigerated	3 days
Meats	Tightly covered, refrigerated	2 days

LEFTOVERS AND OPENED PACKAGED FOODS

ITEM	HOW TO STORE	MAXIMUM STORAGE TIME
Poultry	Stuffing removed and packaged separately, tightly covered and refrigerated	2 days
Salad Dressing	In original container, refrigerated	3 months
Salads, Prepared	Tightly covered, refrigerated	2 days
Seafood	Tightly covered, refrigerated	2 days
Soups & Stocks	Tightly covered, refrigerated	2 days
Stews & Casseroles	Tightly covered, refrigerated	3 days
Wine, red	Tightly corked, at cool room temperature	2-3 days
Wine, white	Tightly corked, refrigerated	3 days

DRY PACKAGED GOODS

ITEM	HOW TO STORE	MAXIMUM STORAGE TIME
Baking Powder & Soda	Airtight, at room temperature	1½ years
Breads & Rolls	Wrapped, at room temperature	3 days
Canned Goods	In cupboard, at room temperature	1 year
Coffee, beans	Airtight, in refrigerator or freezer	2 months
Coffee, ground	Airtight, in refrigerator or freezer	1-2 weeks

DRY PACKAGED GOODS

ITEM	HOW TO STORE	MAXIMUM STORAGE TIME
Cookies & Crackers	Unopened; eat within 1 week of opening	3-4 months
Flours	Airtight, at room temperature	6 months
Fruit, dried	Airtight, at room temperature	6 months
Gelatin, powdered	Airtight, at room temperature	1½ years
Herbs & Spices	Airtight, at room temperature	6 months-1 year
Honey & Syrup	Airtight, at room temperature	1 year
Jam & Jelly	Refrigerate when opened	1 year
Oils	Airtight, at cool room temperature	3 months
Pasta	Airtight, at room temperature	1 year
Peanut Butter	Refrigerate after opening	2 months
Rice, brown	Airtight, at room temperature	1 year
Rice, white	Airtight, at room temperature	2 years
Rice, wild	Airtight, at room temperature	1 year
Shortening	Airtight, at room temperature	6-8 months
Tea	Airtight, at room temperature	6 months

CREATIVE FREEZING GUIDELINES

PLANNING

Develop a plan based on your family favorites and your own entertainment needs. Think of your freezer as a creative tool, not merely a storehouse for leftovers. Don't be a hoarder; keep the inventory changing.

Take a slow day to grate cheese, cook stock, toast croutons, chop onions or make a stack of crepes for freezing. When you get a good buy on mushrooms, make duxelles.

Freeze in meal-size quantities whether for family or bigger occasions. For meat, figure a quarter pound boned per person. If the meat has bones, allow half a pound per person. (Put extra freezer paper over the bone ends to prevent punctures in the wrapping.)

Keep an inventory; it will help you plan menus. If you have a big freezer, the list should also be a record of the contents of each section.

As part of your record-keeping, label every package you put in the freezer. With a felt-tip pen or wax pencil, note the contents and freezing date. You might want to add "reheat at 375°F" or some other instruction.

CREATIVE FREEZING GUIDELINES

PACKAGING

Take a minute to think about the best container for your purpose. Milk cartons are great for storing liquids such as stock, and their rectangular shape makes for easy stacking.

Save little plastic tubs for butters and odds and ends. Plastic bags work well for loose, bulky items like poultry stuffing, and they fit nicely into freezer crannies. The smaller the container, the faster the food will freeze and thaw. When you use gallon containers, fill halfway, cover with a double thickness of freezer paper, then fill the remaining half. For reheating, separate blocks.

Glass freezer jars, which have been tempered for hot and cold, work well, but avoid ordinary glass jars except in a pinch. Freezing makes them brittle.

For party quantities, use big disposable aluminum roasting pans which can go directly into the oven. Pie fillings can also be frozen in the containers in which they'll be baked. If you're short of pie plates and casseroles, freeze the food in the baking dish, then remove it when hard and wrap in plastic or freezer paper. When you're ready to reheat, slip it back into the dish.

Adequate wrapping is the key to successful freezing. All foods should have an airtight seal. Be sure contents are not hot when placed in bags or cartons, or they will stick together.

Take extra care with fish, sliced liver and veal. Wrap in plastic first, then in freezer foil to conserve flavor.

For large pieces of meat like sirloin or chuck roast, put a thin coat of vegetable oil on the cut surface to seal in the juices and prevent freezer burn.

Wrap cakes in foil, plastic wrap, plastic bags or freezer paper. After they're hard, put them in strong cartons or in metal or plastic containers to avert squashing. To prevent damage to the top crust, cover a pie with a paper plate before wrapping. Store cookies in coffee or shortening cans.

FREEZING AND DEFROSTING

Flash (quick) freezing is preferred for pie shells and soft, small items to avoid crushing and save space. Place foods on a metal baking sheet without touching one another and set in the coldest section, freezing as quickly as possible. When solid, stack or scoop into a plastic bag or coffee can.

Don't freeze too much at a time. Crowding puts enough

STORING FOOD

CREATIVE FREEZING GUIDELINES

strain on the motor to render the freezer inefficient. Allow three to four pounds per cubic foot. Freezing takes from two to twenty-four hours, depending on the density of the food, package size and the amount to be frozen. Place packaged, cooled food in contact with the freezer surface. This speeds the process and minimizes flavor loss.

When you are preparing dishes specifically for freezing, undercook slightly. Reheating will bring them to their optimum state.

Do not refreeze food that has been cooked, frozen and reheated. A second reheating would overcook. In addition, as the food sits in the serving dish for a second time, then cools to go back to the freezer, bacteria can flourish.

When in doubt as to whether you may safely refreeze defrosted foods, here's a good rule to follow: Food that has been defrosted in the refrigerator and has not reached more than 40°F (ordinary refrigerator temperature) can safely be refrozen as long as color, odor and texture seem acceptable to you. This is a good thing to remember in case a power failure or other problems cause your freezer to break down.

Poultry or meat which has been frozen uncooked can be refrozen after cooking. Use refrozen foods as soon as possible. In general, a month's storage is safe for cooked foods. Soup stock as well as meat and poultry in liquid will last six months. Use sliced roasted meat and poultry within two weeks.

Shellfish spoil quickly after thawing. Since it's hard to detect spoilage either by odor or appearance, don't refreeze.

After you take things out of the freezer, you'll want to defrost some and cook others frozen. Don't defrost roasts before cooking. Instead, allow about twice the cooking time and cook at low temperature. After the meat has cooked enough to allow insertion of a thermometer, continue roasting until the desired temperature is reached. For juicier hamburgers, broil while still frozen. Meat to be breaded or deep-fried must be thawed first.

Don't bother to thaw cooked frozen stews before reheating. Keep covered while heating. Raw poultry should be thawed slowly before cooking except when making soup, in which case the chicken will thaw in the cooking liquid.

Some sauced dishes may need thickening after thawing. Add a little cornstarch or potato starch to a dab of sauce. Cook, then add to the dish.

Kitchen Measurements and Conversions

It seems sometimes as if no two recipes ever measure things in quite the same way. These quick reference charts—which can be read either left-to-right or right-to-left—should help eliminate some of the confusion.

STANDARD U.S. KITCHEN MEASUREMENTS	
DASH, speck or few grains	less than ⅛ teaspoon
60 DROPS	1 teaspoon
3 TEASPOONS (½ fluid ounce)	1 tablespoon
⅛ CUP (1 fluid ounce)	2 tablespoons
¼ CUP (2 fluid ounces)	4 tablespoons
⅓ CUP	5 tablespoons plus 1 teaspoon
½ CUP (4 fluid ounces)	8 tablespoons
⅔ CUP	10 tablespoons plus 2 teaspoons
¾ CUP (6 fluid ounces)	12 tablespoons

STANDARD U.S. KITCHEN MEASUREMENTS	
1 CUP (8 fluid ounces)	16 tablespoons
2 CUPS (16 fluid ounces)	1 pint
4 CUPS (32 fluid ounces)	1 quart
2 PINTS	1 quart
2 QUARTS	½ gallon
4 QUARTS (liquid)	1 gallon
8 QUARTS (dry)	1 peck
4 PECKS	1 bushel
16 OUNCES (dry measure)	1 pound

A GUIDE TO DOUBLING RECIPES

Many recipes take to being doubled or tripled quite easily. That holds true for most soups, stews, casseroles, salads, dressings and sauces.

However, be aware that seasonings in these dishes do not automatically increase by the same amounts. That is because it doesn't take much spice to permeate an entire dish. If you triple the number of chilies in your favorite Tex-Mex chili, the result will be inedible. So before dumping in that extra cayenne, cumin and the like, taste and adjust the seasonings carefully.

Some things are just not practical to increase. Reduced sauces (those that boil a large amount of liquid down to a concentrated essence) would take too long if you start with twice the amount—especially because many of them must be done right before serving. Trying to knead a double amount of bread dough would be very awkward, as would finding a large enough bowl in which to let it rise. Both of those things are almost always better done in single-recipe amounts.

The more fragile pies, cakes and pastries should also usually be left alone. If you did try doubling, the additional flour would make it necessary to work the dough more. This would increase the amount of gluten developed and would, in turn, mean a tougher result.

And it's one thing if you intend to divide the dough or batter among several pans, but another if you want to put it all in something larger. Not only is it difficult to find a pan that is exactly twice as large as the one called for in the original recipe, but the baking time and temperature would most likely need to change as well. For the average recipe, it would take too much trial and error to determine the appropriate time and temperature. The easiest thing to do for baked goods is to make the same thing twice. That way the results will be guaranteed.

METRIC CONVERSIONS (approximate)	
1/8 TEASPOON	0.5 ml
1/4 TEASPOON	1.5 ml
1/2 TEASPOON	3 ml
3/4 TEASPOON	4 ml
1 TEASPOON	5 ml
1 TABLESPOON	15 ml
1/4 CUP	60 ml
1/3 CUP	85 ml
1/2 CUP	125 ml
1 CUP	250 ml
1 OUNCE (weight)	28 g
1/2 POUND	225 g
3/4 POUND	340 g
1 POUND	450 g

SUBSTITUTIONS AND EQUIVALENTS	
BAKING POWDER, 1 teaspoon	1 teaspoon cream of tartar plus 1/4 teaspoon baking soda
BAKING POWDER	1 teaspoon will leaven 1 cup flour
BREADCRUMBS, 1/3 cup	1 slice of bread
BUTTER or margarine, 2 tablespoons	1 ounce
1/2 cup (4 ounces)	1 stick
1 cup	7/8 to 1 cup vegetable shortening
CHOCOLATE, unsweetened, 1 square	1 ounce
1 square	3 to 4 tablespoons cocoa plus 1 tablespoon shortening
COCONUT, 1 cup grated	1 1/3 cups flaked
CORNSTARCH, 1 tablespoon	2 tablespoons all-purpose flour
CREAM, heavy (40%), 1 cup	3/4 cup milk plus 1/3 cup butter

MEASUREMENTS AND CONVERSIONS

SUBSTITUTIONS AND EQUIVALENTS

CREAM, light (20%), 1 cup	⅞ cup milk plus 3 tablespoons butter
EGGS, whole, 4 to 6	1 cup
whites, 9 to 11	1 cup
yolks, 12 to 14	1 cup
FLOUR, cake, 1 cup sifted	⅞ cup all-purpose flour
GARLIC, 1 clove	¼ teaspoon minced garlic
GELATIN, 1 tablespoon	1 envelope
HERBS, fresh, 1 tablespoon chopped	1 teaspoon dried
LEMON, 1 teaspoon juice	½ teaspoon white vinegar
1 teaspoon grated peel	½ teaspoon lemon extract
MILK, 1 cup whole	½ cup evaporated plus ½ cup water
MUSHROOMS, 1 pound fresh	12 ounces canned, drained
SUGAR, granulated, 2¼ cups	1 pound

SUBSTITUTIONS AND EQUIVALENTS

superfine, 2⅓ cups	1 pound
brown, about 2¼ cups firmly packed	1 pound
granulated brown, about 3⅛ cups	1 pound
confectioners', about 3½ cups	1 pound
SYRUP, corn or maple, about 1½ cups	1 pound
corn, or honey, 1 cup	1¼ cups granulated sugar plus ¼ cup water or milk
TOMATO JUICE, 1 cup	½ cup tomato sauce plus ½ cup water
YOGURT, 1 cup	1 cup buttermilk

YIELDS

BANANAS, 2 to 3 medium	about 1 cup mashed
BEANS AND LENTILS, dried, 1 pound	5 to 6 cups cooked
BREAD, 1-pound loaf	10 cups small bread cubes
BUTTER, 1 pound	3 cups whipped

MEASUREMENTS AND CONVERSIONS

MEASUREMENTS AND CONVERSIONS

YIELDS	
CABBAGE, 1 pound	about 4 cups shredded
CHEESE, 2½ cups freshly grated	½ pound
COFFEE, ground, 1 pound	about 46 six-ounce cups brewed
CREAM, heavy (40%), 1 cup	2 cups whipped
LEMON, 1 whole	2 to 3 tablespoons juice plus 2 teaspoons peel
NUTS, shelled, ¼ pound	1 cup, chopped
ORANGE, 1 medium	about ½ cup juice
PASTA, dried, 1 pound	6 to 8 cups cooked
PEAS, fresh in pods, 1 pound	about 1 cup shelled
POTATOES, 1 pound	about 1¾ cups mashed
RICE, white, 2 cups uncooked	about 5½ cups cooked
TEA LEAVES, 1 pound	about 200 cups brewed
WALNUTS IN THE SHELL, 1 pound	about 2 cups shelled

SUBSTITUTIONS FOR LIGHTER COOKING

REGULAR VERSION	LIGHTER VERSION
Sauteing seafood, meat or poultry in butter or oil	Poaching or steaming them
Dark-meat poultry with skin	White meat without skin
Tuna packed in oil	Tuna packed in water
Sauteing aromatic vegetables in butter or oil	Sweating them with very little fat in a covered nonstick pan over low heat
Thickening sauces with a flour-and-butter roux	Thickening by reduction, or with vegetable purees or cornstarch
Enriching sauces with an egg yolk-and-cream mixture	Using lowfat milk and cornstarch
Whole milk in recipes	Lowfat milk
Sour cream for enrichment or garnish	Lowfat yogurt or buttermilk
Mayonnaise in dressings	Reduced-calorie mayonnaise or lowfat yogurt
Whole-milk cheeses	Part-skim-milk cheeses
Unsweetened chocolate to flavor desserts	Unsweetened cocoa powder
Sugar to sweeten baked goods	Fructose, which has the same calories per spoonful but is sweeter—so you can use ⅓ as much

The Well-Equipped Kitchen

It's amazing how many cooks "make do" with less-than-adequate kitchen equipment. Depending on your own style of cooking, you may not need every single piece of equipment on the checklist that follows; and a visit to any well-equipped kitchen or gourmet shop will reveal many more items than those listed. But if you use this list as your basic guide to equipping your kitchen, you'll certainly be well on the way toward cooking with greater convenience and accuracy.

Preparation Tools

- ❑ Measuring cups
- ❑ Measuring spoons
- ❑ Kitchen scale
- ❑ Mixing bowls (glass, stainless steel or plastic)
  - ❑ Large
  - ❑ Medium
  - ❑ Small
- ❑ Thermometers
  - ❑ Meat thermometer
  - ❑ Oven thermometer
  - ❑ Candy/deep-frying thermometer
  - ❑ Freezer thermometer
- ❑ Kitchen knives
  - ❑ Chef's knife, 8-9 inches
  - ❑ Paring knife
  - ❑ Serrated bread knife
  - ❑ Carving knife
  - ❑ Sharpening steel
- ❑ Cutting board
- ❑ Swivel-blade vegetable parer
- ❑ Kitchen scissors
- ❑ Grater/shredder
- ❑ Pepper mill
- ❑ Nutcracker
- ❑ Openers
  - ❑ Bottle opener
  - ❑ Church key can opener
  - ❑ Rotary can opener
  - ❑ Jar opener
  - ❑ Corkscrew
- ❑ Egg beater or wire whisk
- ❑ Funnel
- ❑ Strainer
- ❑ Colander/drainer
- ❑ Juicer
- ❑ Salad spinner

THE WELL-EQUIPPED KITCHEN

COOKING UTENSILS

- Stock pot
- Saucepans
  - Large (3-quart)
  - Medium (2-quart)
  - Small (1-quart)
- Skillets
  - Large (12-inch)
  - Medium (10-inch)
  - Small (8-inch)
- Wok
- Steamer
- Double boiler
- Kettle
- Heatproof casseroles
  - Large (6-quart)
  - Medium (5-quart)
  - Small (3-quart)
- Shallow baking dishes
- Roasting pans
- Ring molds
  - Large
  - Small
- Wooden spoons
- Rubber spatula
- Metal spatula
- Pancake turner
- Slotted spoon
- Ladle
- Two-pronged cooking fork
- Kitchen tongs
- Skewers
- Bulb baster
- Basting brush

BAKING EQUIPMENT

- Sifter
- Pastry blender
- Pastry scraper
- Rolling pin
- Cake pans
  - 8-inch rounds
  - 9-inch rounds
  - 8- or 9-inch square
  - 9x12-inch
  - Tube pan
- Loaf pans
  - 9x5x3-inch
  - 8½x4½x2½-inch
- Jelly roll pan
- Springform pan
- Cookie cutters
- Cookie sheets
- Muffin tins
- Pie pans
  - 8-inch
  - 9-inch

- Soufflé dish (2-quart)
- Custard or small souffle cups
- Wire cooling rack
- Pastry bag

SMALL APPLIANCES

- Coffee grinder
- Coffee maker
- Electric blender
- Electric mixer
- Hand mixer
- Toaster
- Toaster oven
- Waffle iron
- Food processor *(see sidebar)*
- Electric deep-fryer
- Electric juicer
- Microwave oven *(see sidebar)*

STORAGE, CLEANUP AND CONVENIENCE

- Airtight canisters
- Plastic refrigerator and freezer containers
- Aluminum foil
- Plastic wrap
- Waxed paper
- Paper towels
- Cloth kitchen towels
- Potholders
- Apron

THE WELL-EQUIPPED KITCHEN

Working with Food Processors and Microwave Ovens

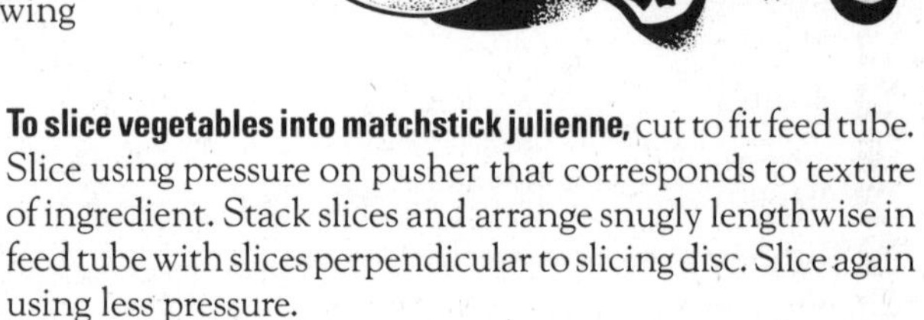

More than any culinary inventions of the century, two appliances—the food processor and the microwave oven—have virtually revolutionized the way we all cook. This revolution of speed and convenience has come along so quickly that it has left a generation of cooks who—while they certainly use and appreciate these two appliances on an almost daily basis—do not necessarily fully understand them or how best to use them.

For best results when using your own machines, keep the following guidelines in mind:

FOOD PROCESSOR

To slice vegetables, cut to fit the feed tube depending on desired result. Standing ingredients such as carrots in feed tube will produce rounds; arranging them lengthwise will produce long, wide slivers. Pack tightly. Pressure on pusher should correspond to texture of ingredient. Use firm pressure on carrots and onions; medium on leeks and zucchini; light pressure on mushrooms.

To slice vegetables into matchstick julienne, cut to fit feed tube. Slice using pressure on pusher that corresponds to texture of ingredient. Stack slices and arrange snugly lengthwise in feed tube with slices perpendicular to slicing disc. Slice again using less pressure.

To mince small items such as garlic, onion, shallots, chilies or ginger, drop through feed tube into dry work bowl with machine running. Process until pieces stop bouncing. Use steel knife.

FOOD PROCESSOR

To chop vegetables, use on/off turns for best control. Check texture frequently. Use steel knife.

To puree ingredients, process until completely smooth, about 2 minutes. Stop occasionally to scrape down sides of work bowl. Use steel knife.

To make meatballs or meat loaf, cut meat into 1-inch cubes. Combine with any other ingredients and process up to 1 pound at a time. Use steel knife.

To chop nuts, place up to two cups nuts in dry work bowl. Chop using on/off turns until desired texture, checking frequently. Use steel knife.

To process bread into fine crumbs, break into quarters. Process up to five slices at a time until as fine as desired. Extra crumbs can be frozen and used directly from the freezer.

To chop cheese, remove any hard outer rind. Cut into 1-inch cubes. Process up to two cups at a time. Chop cheese, using six or eight on/off turns, then process continuously until as fine as desired. Hard cheeses take longer than semisoft ones. Use steel knife.

To shred hard cheeses, bring to room temperature. Remove any hard outer rind; cut into 2-inch pieces. Arrange in feed tube and shred using light pressure. Use shredder.

To melt chocolate in a processor, heat butter or other liquid and keep at simmer. Break chocolate into pieces. Chop chocolate with any sugar using on/off turns, then process continuously until very fine. With machine running, pour hot butter through feed tube and process continuously until chocolate is completely melted and smooth, stopping occasionally to scrape down sides of work bowl with spatula. Use steel knife.

To make crumb toppings or crusts, cut chilled butter into tablespoon-size pieces. Process ingredients until butter is size of small peas. Use steel knife.

To fold dry ingredients into cake batter, spoon dry ingredients in circle onto batter. Blend just until incorporated, using on/off turns; do not overprocess. Use steel knife.

To mix and knead bread dough, first combine dry ingredients in work bowl. With machine running, pour liquid through feed tube and process until dough cleans sides of work bowl. Stop processor to check texture: It should be moist and slightly tacky, but not so wet that it sticks to your hand. If

FOOD PROCESSORS AND MICROWAVE OVENS

dough sticks to bowl, add more flour through feed tube 1 tablespoon at a time, incorporating each addition before adding next. If dough is dry, add water through feed tube 1 teaspoon at a time, incorporating each addition before adding next. Knead by processing until smooth and elastic, about 40 seconds. Kneading takes anywhere from 30 to 90 seconds. Doughs with a high whole-grain content take longer to knead than doughs made with white flour. Use plastic dough blade or steel knife.

To clean batter or dough from steel knife, carefully reinsert blade after work bowl has been emptied and turn machine on for 1 second. The blade will be clean and remaining mixture will adhere to work bowl.

MICROWAVE OVEN

Recipes are often standardized for a 650-watt microwave. If yours has a lower wattage, allow slightly longer cooking times.

Cooking time will be affected by temperature and quantity of food, as well as the size of the dish and the power of the microwave. When recipe specifies a time range, always check at the shortest time to prevent overcooking.

Always use microwave-safe dishes. Most ceramic, glass and earthenware dishes are safe, as are most plastic bowls and containers. Do not use metal, including enameled metalware. China is often safe if it doesn't have metal trim. Items with gold, silver or platinum edging are not recommended. Never use foil trays.

Use the dish size specified in a recipe. If you substitute a different one, the food may not cook as evenly.

Dishes can be covered with microwave-safe lid or plastic wrap. If using plastic wrap, always pierce with a knife to allow steam to escape. Unwrap carefully, away from you.

Food will continue to cook for several minutes after the oven is off; allow sufficient time as recipes direct.

To reheat meat or poultry dishes such as roasts, stews or brisket, cover dish to prevent drying out. Then reheat in short time increments, stopping cooking to check progress. For uniform heating, stir stew or rearrange slices of meat.

To cook boned chicken breasts, wrap each breast half in plastic. Arrange around outer edge of large paper plate. Cook on Medium-High until cooked through, about 5 minutes,

FOOD PROCESSORS AND MICROWAVE OVENS

turning once after 3 minutes. Let stand 5 minutes. Pierce meat through plastic to check doneness. Juices should run clear. If further cooking is required, it is best to cook in 20-second increments.

To cook vegetables, wrap in airtight packets of plastic wrap. Place on paper plate. Cook on High as recipe directs. To test for doneness, pierce vegetables with sharp knife through plastic. Unwrap carefully; mixture will steam.

Sauteing vegetables in the microwave is much like sauteing them stove-top, in terms of both finished result and cooking time.

Cheese melts very quickly in the microwave, because of its high fat content. To soften under-ripe cheeses such as Brie, cook on Medium and rotate several times for even heating. To melt cheese in a liquid, first heat the liquid, then stir in shredded cheese. Return mixture to the microwave and cook until smooth. Cheese does not brown in the microwave; for a browned top, cook in the microwave, then finish under the broiler.

Cooking bacon in the microwave is a snap. It also makes for easy cleanup.

Cooking potatoes in the microwave saves time and energy. You don't have to bring a pot of water to a boil.

To soften chilled butter to room temperature, cut into 4 pieces and arrange in circle on round paper plate, spacing evenly. Cook uncovered on High for 20 to 30 seconds.

To prevent boilover when heating liquids, always use a microwave dish with a capacity three to four times greater than the amount of liquid.

To quick-soak dried ingredients such as chilies and sun-dried tomatoes, place in self-sealing plastic bag with 1 cup hot water; seal bag. (Do not use a twist tie, which contains metal.) Set bag in microwave-safe dish. Cook on High until softened, about 8 minutes.

To plump small dried fruit such as raisins, place in self-sealing plastic bag with any liquid as recipe directs. Seal bag; place in microwave-safe dish. Cook on High until soft, about 2 minutes.

Cooking rice in the microwave doesn't save time—but it does guarantee a perfect result, with no sticking. Less liquid is necessary—usually about ½ cup less for each cup of rice.

MICROWAVE OVEN

To melt chocolate, place in small glass dish. Cook uncovered on Medium for 1 minute, stirring once. If melting chocolate with other ingredients, use High power.

Mixtures that include eggs or egg yolks (but no flour) should be cooked on Medium or Medium-High to prevent curdling. Stir or whisk as recipe directs.

When reheating quick breads such as scones or muffins, wrap in paper towels and place on paper plate. To avoid overheating and steaming, cook in short time increments.

Cake reheats very well in the microwave. Place in microwave-safe dish; do not cover. Always cook on Medium to prevent drying out. A slice of cake will take 50 to 60 seconds, while a whole cake will take 4 to 5 minutes. Do not reheat pies in the microwave; the pastry becomes soggy.

To hasten the first rising of a yeast dough, first test if your microwave can be used. Place one 2-tablespoon piece of refrigerator-cold butter in small dish. Cook uncovered on lowest setting 4 minutes. If butter has melted completely, unit is too hot and should not be used. If *most* of butter has melted (some solids should remain), unit can be used. Place dough in 2-quart bowl; coat dough lightly with oil. Cover loosely with plastic. Half fill large bowl with hot tap water. Set bowl with dough into bowl of water. Cook on lowest setting 4 minutes. Let rest in microwave 12 minutes. Repeat sequence 1 or 2 more times as necessary, until dough has doubled.

Entertaining Tips

Does it ever seem to you as if certain people you know are just born hosts or hostesses, always effortlessly throwing perfect parties? Whether it comes naturally to them or not, people who throw great parties—whether intimate gatherings or grand galas—follow a few basic principles that ensure success. Here's the lowdown:

PLAN CAREFULLY. Give yourself plenty of time to finalize the guest list, issue invitations (whether by mail or phone), and plan the menu. You might want to keep a record of each party you throw, so you can refer back to see what worked, who got along—or didn't—with whom, and so on.

KNOW YOUR STYLE. Suit the party not only to the occasion but to the guests, the surroundings, and to you yourself. If you're more comfortable in the casual mode, maybe an ultra-formal dinner party isn't such a good idea. A weekend gathering at a beach house calls for a different approach than, say, a weeknight supper in a city apartment. If you enjoy hanging out in your kitchen, plan the party so it happens there rather than out in the dining room.

GIVE SPECIAL THOUGHT TO THE MENU. Concentrate on fresh seasonal foods. Consider your guests and any special likes, dislikes or dietary needs they might have. Balance the menu between simple and complex tastes and preparations. Consider, too, what plates or bowls you might serve different dishes in; a particularly beautiful piece might itself inspire a recipe.

CONSIDER TIMING. Plan out the most sensible and convenient order of preparation for your menu. As much as possible, prepare whole dishes or parts of recipes in advance, with the final assembly or cooking to take place as guests arrive or just before serving.

GIVE NEW RECIPES A DRY RUN. If you're planning to serve some new, challenging dish, you might want to try making the recipe for yourself and your family, to make sure you're happy with the results.

PAY ATTENTION TO THE SETTING. Set the table to suit the style of the occasion and the food. Give your imagination free reign in creating a centerpiece—whether cut flowers or potted plants, baskets of bread and fruit or an assortment of blazing candles, unusual folk art curios or a collection of seaside rocks and shells. According to your preference, use matching tableware and cutlery or an attractive jumble of styles.

PAY ATTENTION TO YOUR GUESTS. Never lose sight of the fact that your guests—rather than the food—are the true focal point of the evening. First and foremost, pay attention to their needs. If you think it's appropriate, plan the seating in advance to match up guests for lively conversation; then have them change their places and partners for the dessert course, to encourage maximum mingling.

Matching Wine with Food

There's no real secret to choosing the right wines to go with the foods you serve. Your selection, like any other cooking or menu-planning decision, will depend in large part on how you want the flavors of the wine and the food to complement or contrast with each other. The following simple guidelines may help you:

RED WITH MEAT, WHITE WITH FISH. It's probably the most widely repeated piece of wine advice, and there's some truth to it. Seafoods, being lighter in flavor and texture, call for the lightness of white wines—from the simple, crisp quality of a Chablis or Sauvignon Blanc to accompany delicate fish like sole or snapper, to the greater complexity of a Chardonnay as a companion to richer seafood like salmon or lobster. Beef, lamb and pork call for more robust red wines such as Cabernet, Pinot Noir or Zinfandel. Poultry, depending on how it's prepared, can go with either a white or a red wine.

LET THE SAUCE HELP YOU DECIDE. If a particular kind of wine goes into the sauce for a dish, that same variety would be appropriate to serve alongside it. If a sauce is particularly creamy or scented with sweet herbs or other flavorings, opt for a fruitier, sweeter wine—say a Riesling or a Gewurztraminer—over a drier one. Serve a brisk red wine such as a Beaujolais or a Chianti with tomato-based sauces whose acidity might mask a more delicate white wine.

APPROPRIATE CHOICES FOR ETHNIC CUISINES. Don't shy away from matching wine with cuisines other than those that traditionally call for it. Again, let simple taste-matching principles apply. Crisp white wines go well with seafood-based cuisines like Japanese or Cantonese. Spicier cooking—from Szechuan to Southeast Asian, Indian to Mexican—calls for a robust red wine like a Zinfandel, or a fruity, spicy white such as a Gewurztraminer; more subtly seasoned dishes in these cuisines could call for a refreshing white wine such as Sauvignon Blanc.

BEND THE RULES IF YOU WANT TO. Do you really love Chardonnay? Then there's no reason you can't bend the rules a little. A big, buttery-flavored Chardonnay has enough body and complexity to stand up to a simply grilled steak. For that matter, a light red wine, slightly chilled, would taste just fine with salmon. In the end, it's your own enjoyment of the food-and-wine experience that matters most, so follow your personal preferences as much as you follow the rules.

AN AMERICAN WINE GLOSSARY

In recent years, the vineyards of California and other American wine-producing regions have won world-class renown. And their availability as a home-grown product has made wine a more integral part of the nation's dining tables than ever before.

The following brief descriptions of the most common American wine varieties may help you in your choice of the right wine for the right dish.

BLUSH WINES. A generic description for white wines made from such red-skinned grapes as Cabernet Sauvignon, Pinot Noir and Zinfandel. Noted for its faint pink color and a light, delicate fruitiness.

CABERNET SAUVIGNON. A rich, big red wine noted for its signature flavor of black or red currants.

CHARDONNAY. Among the richest of white wines, dry yet fruity, often displaying a buttery character and with the oaklike quality of the barrels in which it is often aged.

GEWURZTRAMINER. Softly sweet and spicy, this white wine is often noted for its fresh taste of honeydew melons.

JOHANNISBERG RIESLING. A fresh-tasting, fruity and slightly sweet white wine reminiscent of apples and melons.

MERLOT. A soft, gentle, medium-bodied red wine.

PETITE SIRAH. Spicy and robust, this red wine has a simple, casual character.

PINOT NOIR. This complex, elegant red wine is appreciated for its almost ethereal refinement.

SAUVIGNON BLANC. A crisp, full-flavored white wine with a citrus-like character that may be compared to lemon or grapefruit.

ZINFANDEL. Smooth yet spicy, the flavor of this bold, dry red wine is often compared to blackberries.

MATCHING WINE WITH FOOD

STOCKING THE BAR

Nowadays, fewer and fewer people are indulging in alcoholic beverages. But a bar well stocked with both soft and hard drinks is still an important part of any serious home entertaining.

The following checklist will help you stock a bar that can easily handle up to 50 guests; you may want to alter the contents depending on your knowledge of your guests' individual tastes. Check your bar inventory against the list regularly to make sure that supplies never run low.

SOFT DRINKS AND MIXERS

- ☐ Cola and diet cola (4 quarts)
- ☐ Ginger ale (3 quarts)
- ☐ Tonic (8 quarts)
- ☐ Club soda (8 quarts)
- ☐ Mineral water (2 six-packs)
- ☐ Juices (3 quarts, plus assorted single-serving bottles or cans)
- ☐ Nonalcoholic beer (2 six-packs)

ALCOHOLIC DRINKS

- ☐ Beer and light beer (2 cases)
- ☐ White wine (12 bottles)
- ☐ Red wine (3 bottles)
- ☐ Champagne (2 bottles California; 1 bottle French)
- ☐ Brandy or Cognac (1 fifth)
- ☐ Scotch (3 quarts domestic; 1 fifth imported)
- ☐ Canadian blended whisky (1 fifth)
- ☐ Bourbon and Tennessee sour mash (2 quarts)
- ☐ Vodka (3 quarts domestic; 2 fifths imported)
- ☐ Gin (1 quart domestic; 1 fifth imported)
- ☐ Tequila (1 fifth)
- ☐ Light rum (1 fifth)
- ☐ Golden or dark rum (1 fifth)
- ☐ Dry vermouth (1 fifth)
- ☐ Sweet vermouth (1 fifth)
- ☐ Campari (2 fifths)
- ☐ Pernod (1 fifth)
- ☐ White Dubonnet or Lillet (2 fifths)
- ☐ Creme de cassis (1 small bottle)

ODDS AND ENDS

- ☐ Ice (6 ten-pound bags)
- ☐ Lemons
- ☐ Limes
- ☐ Olives

ALL ABOUT COFFEE

COFFEE VARIETIES AND ROASTS. Coffee beans—not beans at all but the pit of a cherrylike fruit from an evergreen tree—come from many parts of the world. From Central and South America, in addition to Brazil's enormous crop (used mostly for blending), there are mellow Colombian, mild Costa Rican and richly aromatic Antiguan from Guatemala. From East and West Africa, connoisseurs search out rich, clean-tasting Kenyan and exotic Ethiopian. Indonesia produces Java (a name that has long been synonymous with fine coffee) and fine Celebes Kalossi. The West Indies trees contribute, among others, Jamaican Blue Mountain, a coffee as rare as a Vermeer. The only coffee produced in the United States is the Kona variety, grown on the slopes of Hawaiian volcanoes.

Most coffee is made from two varieties of beans: the aristocratic *arabica*, which is grown at high altitudes and produces all the finest coffees, and the blander *robusta* used mostly for instant coffees and for blending.

Trial by fire in a roasting machine produces roasts from the lightest cinnamon color through the darkest espresso. In *The Signet Book of Coffee and Tea*, Peter Quimme says that full city roast is the ideal one, its chestnut color confirming that the beans are at the maximum development of their rich, genuine flavor. Darker roast coffees range from Viennese through French and almost black Italian, which has the strongest flavor and slightly less caffeine than lighter roasts. If you're in search of a caffeine-free coffee, try decaffeinated Colombian or French roasts, which have the same flavor as their kickier siblings but have been freed, by means of a chemical or organic solvent, of the physiological effects of caffeine.

TO MAKE THE PERFECT CUP OF COFFEE. First, match the grind to the method: Percolators use regular grind, automatic electric drip and filter cones take drip, vacuum coffee makers a fine grind and espresso pots a very fine grind. Always use two level tablespoons of coffee to six ounces of freshly drawn cold water newly brought to the boil (the only exception is in double-strength coffees such as *café filtre* and espresso, and for them you use twice as much coffee). Too much coffee makes a bitter brew, too little a weak one, so if you think your coffee is too strong, dilute it with hot water after brewing or try a lighter roast.

ALL ABOUT COFFEE

The best way to make coffee is with the quick and easy drip method, while the ubiquitous American percolator wins the prize for making the absolute worst. It either boils the coffee or fails to heat it enough or extends the eight-minute brewing cycle, extracting oils mercilessly from the beans and producing a bitter parboiled liquid. Other methods that produce a good cup of coffee include vacuum pots, plunger pots like the French Melior, cold water steeping, which produces a concentrate, or espresso machines. The pot must be absolutely clean, since oils and residues can affect the brewing. Don't use a large pot to make small amounts and do serve the coffee immediately.

KEEPING BEANS FRESH. No matter how careful your preparation and how fine your machine, it will all be for nothing if the beans or ground coffee aren't fresh. Once beans are roasted, most retain their freshness for only about three weeks: Darker French and Italian roasts have a somewhat longer life. Once ground, all beans begin to lose their flavor immediately and are at their best for only four or five days. Unopened vacuum-packed coffee stays fresh for months; once the can is opened, the same figures apply. For the freshest coffee, either buy ground coffee in small quantities or grind the beans at home as you need them. Store beans in an airtight canister at room temperature or in an airtight glass jar with rubber seal in the refrigerator or freezer.

Then all you need is some cold water and expectant taste buds as you set off on the adventure of finding coffees you like. A clear, clean-flavored blend containing Colombian is a favorite choice of many for breakfast; Kona, Brazilian Santos, East African and Central American are other preferred varieties. In the evening, the dark-roasted French and Italian coffees are popular.

Don't be afraid to experiment in the wonderland of beans and blends.

ALL ABOUT TEA

VARIETIES AND BLENDS. Whether you are planning an elaborate tea ceremony or just contemplating a simple potful with friends, the varieties of tea are many. But no matter if it is called Darjeeling, Formosa Oolong or Dragon Well, all tea comes from one plant, an evergreen shrub of the camellia family, which grows best in tropical and subtropical climates. Though the plant prefers warm, wet days, it will grow almost anywhere; and tea grown at higher, cooler altitudes, much like high-grown coffees, is often considered the finest by tea connoisseurs.

Despite the many varieties and blends, there are really only three kinds of tea—black, oolong and green. It is the processing the determines their differences. Processing is either a three- or four-step operation. First, *withering* removes as much moisture as possible from the leaves. Then *rolling* breaks up the cell structure of the dried leaves and releases their natural juices and fragrances. Third, *fermentation* (actually a misleading technical term for the process of oxidation) exposes the leaves to air; the oxygen they absorb changes the color of the leaves from green to copper or black. Finally, they are *dried* or *fired*, which stops the oxidation process and dries the leaves evenly.

Black tea, which accounts for almost 97 percent of the tea drunk in the United States, is subjected to all four processing steps. Darjeeling, Keemun and Ceylon are black teas. A well-brewed black tea will have a rich, strong flavor and mellow aroma.

Oolong teas are lightly withered and rolled and only partially fermented before being dried; the leaves are half copper, half black. Not as strong as black tea, oolong is rich and fruity tasting.

Green teas are not fermented. The leaves are steamed or heated rather than withered, then rolled and dried. The leaves remain green because they do not oxidize. Green tea is light and clear with a delicate, flavorful taste.

Black tea is graded by the size of the leaf and divided into classes that are not indicative of flavor or quality. Orange pekoe, which many people mistakenly assume to be a variety of tea, is made up of long, thin black leaves; pekoe, the shorter, not as wiry leaves; and pekoe souchong, the largest, rounded leaves. The whole leaves need a longer brewing time, while the broken leaves (about 80 percent of the crop) make a stronger, darker pot of tea in less time. The broken grades are usually considered the choice teas, especially in the

ALL ABOUT TEA

United States where they are the essential tea for tea bags. Green teas are graded according to the style of drying as well as the size of the leaves.

Though processing produces only three types of finished tea, there are in fact dozens of varieties, usually named for the area in which they are grown, and some 3,000 different blends. Each tea has its own style and grace, its own loyal followers and avid supporters.

Keemun, one of the finest black teas China produces, is complex and subtle, just as good wine is, with a powerful aroma and rich taste. Just the tea for an early morning bracer. From China's Fukien province there's Lapsang Souchong, smoky and exotic. Dragon Well, the rarest of China's green teas and one of the legendary teas of the world, is sweet and delicate.

Distinguished Indian teas include rich Darjeeling, the Champagne of teas, grown at the foothills of the Himalayas; and sturdy Assam, a powerful black tea that makes a brisk pungent pot. If you can drink just one oolong, be sure it's Formosa Oolong, picked only once a year in Taiwan. Another rare gem of a tea is Ceylon, blended from the best estates in high growing areas.

Of all the tea varieties, English Breakfast, traditionally a China Keemun, is surely one of the most popular. It got its name from the English habit of adding milk to tea, which brings out its distinctive aroma. Earl Grey, a blend of Indian and Ceylon teas flavored with oil of bergamot, is another popular tea. Legend has it that the recipe for this blend was given to Earl Grey, a British ambassador, by a Chinese mandarin.

Herbal teas, which aren't really teas at all—they don't come from tea plants or have any caffeine—are becoming an increasingly fashionable drink. They are what the French call *tisanes* and are made by pouring boiling water over any variety of dried herbs and spices ranging from verbena, mint leaves, spicy sassafras and astringent rose hips to ginseng, peppermint or soothing camomile. All are said to have beneficial effects—some stimulating, some soothing—on various organs.

HOW TO STORE TEAS. One pound of tea makes approximately 200 cups and most tinned teas last only about one year,

ALL ABOUT TEA

so when you've decided on a variety worthy of investigation, be careful not to buy more than you need. Fine Keemuns and Darjeelings have the best track record for staying fresh, while green teas lose quality very quickly. Loose teas bought from a specialty shop that has a large volume of business will probably be fresher and keep longer than prepackaged teas. Store in lightproof, airtight containers at room temperature.

MAKING THE PERFECT CUP. Though all the curious tea-brewing paraphernalia available could intimidate the novice, making the perfect cup of tea *shouldn't* be difficult: All you need is a teapot and fresh water. Use a clean porcelain or earthenware teapot that has been warmed by filling with hot water for a few minutes. Put one teaspoon of tea per six-ounce cup into it and bring freshly drawn water to a rolling boil. Pour it over the leaves immediately, let it steep for five minutes and serve. Some experts disapprove of tea balls because the leaves can't expand in the water but remain packed in the ball. And many suggest using distilled or spring water if you're not crazy about the source from your local tap. Tea bags, the invention of a New York merchant who filled small silk bags with portions of tea as tasters' samples, are more expensive than loose tea and rarely contain fine blends. But they can make adequate tea if you leave them to steep for the required five minutes.

It's hardly in the refined British custom of tea with milk and sugar, but tea enthusiasts of experimental bent can try their favorite drink in any number of guises, including the very popular iced version. Sun tea, a product of time and energy, requires only one quart of cold water, ten tea bags and a sunny morning. After six hours or so, your tea will be brewed perfectly and ready to pour over ice for a thirst-quenching reviver. Or try tea ice cream made with English Breakfast tea for a deliciously different treat, then use the leaves for a spot of fortune-telling. It might get you into hot water with tea traditionalists, but then, that's precisely where tea leaves belong.

A few recommendations for building a kitchen reference library that will help you meet every challenge and rise to every occasion.

CLASSICS

THE CLASSIC ITALIAN COOK BOOK by Marcella Hazan (Alfred A. Knopf, 1976). Wonderfully readable and greatly varied, the 250 recipes in this collection teach how to cook—and eat—Italian-style.

ENTERTAINING by Martha Stewart (Clarkson N. Potter, 1982). Scores of stylish and casual throw-it-yourself parties, for all occasions and in every room of the house, presented with a wealth of handsome photographs.

JAMES BEARD'S AMERICAN COOKERY by James Beard (Little, Brown, 1972). The late great dean of American cooking referred to this 1,500-recipe exploration of the nation's culinary heritage as "my dictionary."

JOY OF COOKING by Irma S. Rombauer and Marion Rombauer Becker (Bobbs-Merrill, 1975). First published in 1931 and revised in recent years, this indispensable masterpiece includes some 4,500 recipes.

MAIDA HEATTER'S BOOK OF GREAT AMERICAN DESSERTS by Maida Heatter (Alfred A. Knopf, 1985). The Queen of Sweets presents a superb collection of old and new recipes for everybody's favorite course.

MASTERING THE ART OF FRENCH COOKING, volume 1, by Julia Child, Louisette Bertholle and Simone Beck; and volume 2, by Child and Beck (Alfred A. Knopf, 1983). The classic that continues to teach Americans how to cook with the finesse of the French.

MICROWAVE GOURMET by Barbara Kafka (William Morrow, 1987). Voluminous and exhaustive, this ultimate book on microwave cooking is on the cutting edge of contemporary cuisine.

THE NEW YORK TIMES 60-MINUTE GOURMET by Pierre Franey (Times Books, 1979). Culled from the popular column in **THE NEW YORK TIMES,** these quick-and-easy recipes, practical and in good taste, range from the haute to the homey.

THE SILVER PALATE COOKBOOK by Julee Rosso and Sheila Lukins with Michael McLaughlin (Workman Publishing, 1982). A lively collection of quick, easy recipes—complete with tips, hints and how-tos—that's among the most popular titles on contemporary entertaining.

THE KITCHEN BOOKSHELF

HEALTHY EATING

THE COMPLETE BOOK OF FOOD by Carol Ann Rinzler (Pharos Books, 1987). From apples to zucchini, a nutritional profile of each food item, followed by the most nutritious ways to cook and serve.

COOK IT LIGHT by Jeanne Jones (Macmillan, 1987). Healthy recipes that are more imaginative than in most collections of this type.

DIETS DON'T WORK by Bob Schwartz (Breakthrough Publishing, 1986). A psychological approach to losing weight—and keeping it off.

EAT SMART FOR A HEALTHY HEART COOKBOOK by Denton A. Cooley, M.D. and Carolyn E. Moore, Ph.D., R.D. (Barron's, 1987). Very sound principles, with appealing recipes and menus.

HARRIET ROTH'S CHOLESTEROL-CONTROL COOKBOOK by Harriet Roth (New American Library, 1989). Appealing recipes with cosmopolitan flair highlight one of the better books on this very important subject.

MANAGING YOUR MIND AND MOOD THROUGH FOOD by Judith J. Wurtman, Ph.D. (Harper & Row Perennial Library, 1988). Shows how foods can increase concentration, prevent afternoon slumps, ease mood swings, calm stress and anxiety and more.

THE MEDITERRANEAN DIET: WINE, PASTA, OLIVE OIL AND A LONG, HEALTHY LIFE by Carol and Malcolm McConnell (W.W. Norton & Co., 1987). An exploration, with recipes, of why the diet of Mediterranean villagers has long led to a far lower rate of heart disease and cancer than that of the industrial West.

THE NATURAL GOURMET by Annemarie Colbin (Ballantine Books, 1989). A variety of international recipes reflects the author's serious whole-foods approach to cooking.

RODALE'S BASIC NATURAL FOODS COOKBOOK edited by Charles Gerras (Fireside Books, 1989). A reliable basic cookbook with a healthy (not vegetarian) orientation.

THE KITCHEN BOOKSHELF

WINES

AMERICAN WINE: A COMPREHENSIVE GUIDE by Anthony Dias Blue (Harper & Row, 1988). This is the definitive reference source on the subject, covering wineries and wine from all over the United States.

THE BENEFITS OF MODERATE DRINKING by Gene Ford (The Wine Appreciation Guild, 1988). An important work that offers a thorough and well-reasoned response to the growing neo-prohibitionist movement.

CHAMPAGNE by Serena Sutcliffe (Simon & Schuster, 1988). A colorful and thorough volume on the world's most famous sparkling wine.

COGNAC by Nicholas Faith (David R. Godine, 1987). Considered the best book written about this subject.

THE ESSENTIAL WINE BOOK by Oz Clarke (Fireside Books, 1988). An excellent introduction to wine, as well as a good reference.

NOTES ON A CALIFORNIA CELLAR BOOK by Bob Thompson (Beech Tree Books, 1988). A personal and well-written book about California wines, full of insight and intelligence.

RED WINE WITH FISH by David Rosenthal and Joshua Wesson (Simon & Schuster, 1989). The best book yet about putting wine and food together and maximizing the pleasure of this blissful combination.

THINKING ABOUT WINE by Elin McCoy and John Frederick Walker (Simon & Schuster, 1989). This husband-and-wife team challenges some basic assumptions in a thoughtful and often controversial manner.

THROUGH THE GRAPEVINE: THE BUSINESS OF WINE IN AMERICA by Jay Stuller and Glen Martin (Wynwood Press, 1989). A fascinating, behind-the-scenes look at the U.S. wine industry and who controls it.

WINES OF THE GRAVES by Pamela Vandyke Price (The Wine Appreciation Guild, 1988). A serious, comprehensive work on the superb wines of the southernmost region of Bordeaux.

THE KITCHEN BOOKSHELF

INDEX

This index is for both Volume I and Volume II of Bon Appétit's *21st Century Basics*. The volume number precedes the page number for each entry. For example, "Barbecuing tips, II:17" indicates that pointers on barbecuing will be found in Volume II on page 17.

INDEX

INDEX

INDEX

INDEX

INDEX

INDEX

INDEX

INDEX

CREDITS & ACKNOWLEDGMENTS

The following people contributed the text included in this book:

Anthony Dias Blue
Karen Hallal
Zack Hanle
Norman Kolpas
Rita Leinwand
Abby Mandel
Richard Sax
Marie Simmons
Jan Weimer

Concept:
Susan M. Allyn and Wendy J. Weber

Editorial development and original writing:
Norman Kolpas

Graphic design:
Sandy Douglas

Illustrations:
Steve Miller

Production:
Joan Valentine

Index:
Barbara Wurf

Proofreader:
Katie Goldman

Rights and permissions:
Gaylen Ducker